Marriage
is Not for the
Faint of Heart

written by
Adrian and Pamela Stovall

Revised edition© 2017 by Sacred Covenant Ministries

All rights reserved. No part of this book may be reproduced in any form, except for the inclusion of brief quotations in a review, without written permission from the authors.

Unless otherwise indicated, all Scripture quotations are taken from New King James Version®. Copyright © 1982 by Thomas Nelson. Used by permission. All rights reserved.

Other Scripture quotations are as follows:

Amplified Bible (AMP), Copyright © 2015 by The Lockman Foundation. Used by permission.

Holy Bible, New Living Translation (NLT), copyright ©1996, 2004, 2007, 2013, 2015 by Tyndale House Foundation. Used by permission of Tyndale House Publishers, Inc., Carol Stream, Illinois 60188. All rights reserved.

THE MESSAGE (MSG), copyright © 1993, 1994, 1995, 1996, 2000, 2001, 2002 by Eugene H. Peterson. Used by permission of NavPress. All rights reserved. Represented by Tyndale House Publishers, Inc.

New American Standard Bible® (NASB), Copyright © 1960, 1962, 1963, 1968, 1971, 1972, 1973,1975, 1977, 1995 by The Lockman Foundation Used by permission

Amplified® Bible Classic (AMPC), Copyright © 1954, 1958, 1962, 1964, 1965, 1987 by The Lockman Foundation. Used by permission.

New Century Version (NCV). Copyright © 2005 by Thomas Nelson. Used by permission. All rights reserved.

The Holy Bible, English Standard Version® ESV, copyright © 2001 by Crossway, a publishing ministry of Good News Publishers. Used by permission. All rights reserved."

New Life Version (NLV) copyright ©1969 by Christian Literature International. Used by permission.

ISBN: 978-0-9768335-3-6

We dedicate this book to our children, their spouses, and our grandchildren. It is our prayer that you may create an environment of love, acceptance, and forgiveness that emulates Christ's love for the Church and continue to experience God's blessings as you have committed to "Do the Word." It is also our prayer for each of you that God's blessing would be manifested in the production of godly seed who will love God as long as time exists.

Contents

Introduction	vii
1. Marriage: The Televised Version	1
2. Marriage is not for the Faint of Heart	4
3. Marriage is for the Faith Filled	7
4. Marriage: A Gift From God	10
5. The Two Marriage Killers	19
6. Can Love Really Last Forever?	26
7. Being Best Friends	33
8. Dispelling the Myths	46
9. The Dreaded "F" Word	50
10. "I'll Take That"	62
11. The J-J-Joy of S-S-Submission	78
12. Let's Talk	89
13. What God Wants You to Know About Sex	96
14. Take Heart, Be Encouraged	100
Encouraging Marriage Thoughts	103
End notes	302
References	305
Recommended Reading	307

Introduction

Marriage was never meant to be the casual plaything it has become in our society. The attitude now seems to be: "Let me try this marriage thing out for a while; and if it doesn't work out, I'll just get a divorce." Nowadays, divorce is not as stigmatized as it once was, so it's no big deal. But it *is* a big deal. God hasn't changed His feelings about divorce. It is still the breaking of a covenant. It still breaks His heart because it represents brokenness, and a lack of faith in His ability to help and heal a situation we have committed to in His presence. It still represents a tearing apart of a union we have asked Him to join.

It has been our experience over the years that, after much discussion and reasoning with couples and individuals, most people are actually shocked to find out the tremendous amount of hard work a marriage takes. Oddly enough, one of the best descriptive quotes we've heard regarding the challenge of marriage came from a segment in the children's movie, *Spy Kids*, written and directed by Robert Rodriguez. Here the mother, in a bedtime story, is describing how two international spies made the decision to unite as one:

> "...they decided that together they would embark on the most dangerous mission of all times; they decided to marry.
>
> Oh yes, on her wedding day she felt like she would rather

brave a thousand missions than what she was about to attempt. Marriage is a mission that is so complex that only the most courageous (and slightly insane) need apply. There is such an amazing series of obstacles to overcome to keep a marriage together much less a family, and it frightened even her, a hardened and experienced secret agent. But when she saw him standing there with no doubt whatsoever, so assured, so enamored with what they were about to do, she took his hand, looked deep into his eye and said the two most dangerous and trusting words you can say to anyone. She said, "I do."

Having a healthy, eyes-wide-open attitude about marriage will help you avoid many pitfalls. This is the basis of our book: taking a hard, honest look at marriage and doing what it takes to create a healthy, happy, and harmonious home. Unfortunately, when most people say, "I do," they don't bargain for difficulty; they don't expect that to be their personal experience; so naturally, they don't plan for it. And to be perfectly honest, most couples are *not* willing to work *that* hard when they truly understand the challenge. As a result, you wind up with two people who live miserably for a while, then decide to go their separate ways, or two people who exist in the same environment as no more than roommates or business partners. How sad!

It's difficult to believe that when you decided to get married you had your hopes set on having a boring, mundane, lonely life together, or on getting divorced. Of course, you didn't! You were probably starry-eyed and full of hope and anticipation for having found that one person who would complete and share this wonderful journey of life with you. Well, if you see yourself headed in the wrong direction, stop yourself in your tracks right now, and get to work on making the necessary changes!

A word of caution to those who are in the planning stages of matrimony. If you go into a marriage convinced that everything will remain the same, that nothing will change, PLEASE do not get married. You will be devastated! Change is a necessary part of life. Your outlook on life will change. Your bodies will change. Your attitudes will change. Your love will even change. These changes could (and should) be good things; but if you are unprepared for them, they could destroy your marriage.

It is our desire to impart to you God's truths about marriage in both spiritual and practical terms and in a way that will spark the desire to have more than just a *good* marriage but a thriving, exciting one!

1.
Marriage: The Televised Version

Have you ever sat down and really analyzed the TV version of marriage? It's really quite an interesting study, especially television of recent years. Turn on any sitcom and you will see wives treating their husbands like imbeciles or husbands insulting their wives. They play head games with each other. Marriage is represented as sport, pitting spouses against each other, and it's perceived as "normal" for children to speak disrespectfully to their parents.

The unfortunate part of all this is we, as humans, are so influenced by what our eyes see that we begin to imitate the behavior demonstrated on TV. Most disheartening is that it is also seen in Christian marriages. Somehow or another, we have begun to think that biblical principles are now obsolete; that treating each other with respect and honor is somehow "corny."

Recently, while teaching a class, we were discussing communicating and listening. One of the students made the comment that some people aren't happy unless they can get into an argument; that it made them feel alive. Our comment back to him was that they just needed to be retrained. It's true, there are those who believe this is normal, and that's only because it's what has been the example put before them. No one in his right mind would rather have turmoil and tension than peace.

There was a very popular television sitcom that had been on for several seasons and is now in syndication. It depicted a young, married couple whose in-laws lived across the street, and both families were deeply dysfunctional. The younger couple constantly disagreed about almost everything. The wife used sex as a reward and the lack of it as punishment. She oftentimes called him an idiot or some similar term; she was overbearing and insulting. Her husband, on the other hand, was a weak example of a head of household. He tried different types of manipulations to get what he wanted. He whined and complained to no avail as he very rarely got his way. The in-laws were interfering, but the worst of it was that the father-in-law took every opportunity to declare his disdain for marriage. They displayed marriage as bondage and an unpleasant life sentence.

We watched to gain insight, but cringed every time we saw this series. Of course, we realize this was just someone trying to parody marriage, but we also recognized that this is how many Americans view their own marriages. How very sad that marriage has become a laughingstock or viewed as some bizarre form of torture.

We would like to propose to you a very different perspective and version of marriage that represents

God's plan and purpose.[1] We would like to present to you a plan for marriage where the participants are indeed challenged, yet blessed and empowered, to succeed – a union where the members respect, support, encourage, protect, nourish, truly love, and endeavor to make life better because they are united with each other.

God cannot be left out of this marital equation because He is the One Who ordained, endorsed, and sanctioned this plan of unity and has promised to be the "glue factor." He is the One who knows how to make *it and us* work well.

2.

Marriage is not for the Faint of Heart

Also [Jesus] told them a parable to the effect that they ought always to pray and not to turn coward - faint, lose heart and give up (Luke 18:1, AMPC)

Marriage, itself, is a God creation; and as His creation, in order to be successful in it, you *have* to know what the Creator desired and planned for it. And you need the help of the Creator to navigate the issues that will arise.

The dictionary definition for faintheartedness is: cowardly, having lost courage, timid, destitute of courage.[1]

Our world is changing at breakneck speed, but God's Word, never changes. The only tried and true method for a successful marriage is to apply the principles of His Word. Are the only successful marriages those between Christians? Absolutely not! However, we would venture to say that those who are successful have somehow begun applying godly principles, perhaps without even being aware of it.

What are we trying to say? Simply this: God's Word is true and it works; and when you give it first place in your marriage, you will see success you could not have imagined.

Why is marriage not for the faint of heart? Because it requires bold and courageous efforts to resist and defeat the antagonistic forces against marriage that surround us and may even exist within us.

God designed marriage as a blessing and help to mankind; but just as in all good endeavors, there are enemies and adversaries to His plan. Our challenge is to find and receive God's truth concerning marriage, then fight the good fight of faith in order to receive that promised blessing.

Success in your marriage and your life are dependent on you finding truth and turning the truth you find into wisdom. You must then discipline yourself to apply the wisdom you've developed, while allowing God to assist you in the discernment of a God-centered life and marriage.

It takes a great deal of courage to stay and fight for a marriage. And you can't be lazy about it. It's easier to pack it in or acquiesce to something other than your desired goals. Our daughter-in-law said it best, "It takes so much more discipline to stay in there and ask God to change you."

In order to understand that a good marriage is the result of knowing God's Word and applying it, you must first know God's plan and desire for marriage.[2] It is important to begin to search the Word of God for answers to the questions you have regarding your marriage. In fact, the Bible is full of all the instructions you will ever need concerning all the relationships you will have in life. Begin to view the Word as a love manual that needs to be practiced at home with your spouse, first, before you experiment on the world.

3.
Marriage is for the Faith Filled

We have said that marriage is not for the faint of heart because we believe that a successful marriage belongs to the faith-filled couple. Since marriage was the idea and creation of God, as with everything that is God-centered, it is faith based and sustained. By this we believe that the only way to succeed in your marriage is to know what God says about marriage and believe God to bring it to pass in your life, home, and everyday experience.

Faith is a spiritual quality which connects us to the power of God.

*Now faith is the assurance (the confirmation, the title-deed) of things (we) hope for, being the proof of things (we) do not see and the conviction of their reality – faith perceiving as real what is not revealed to the senses (*Heb. 11:1 AMPC). Faith is an assurance of the heart that is more than mere mental assent to certain information or promises. God's promises are unchanging, spiritual realities regardless of whether we are experiencing them or not. Your faith will allow you to receive and be assured of the reality of God's promises and have peace, patience, and commitment to continue. Your faith will allow you to continue even in the face of contrary, physical evidence.

This is why it so important that you know the promises of God concerning marriage so that you place your faith in God to deliver His will and plan for your life. Conducting your relationship by faith is walking by the Word and basing your actions and judgments upon what the Bible says concerning your situation. Many couples pray for their relationship without knowing what God's plan is for marriage. God desires for marriage to be a blessing that causes you to praise, and worship Him for His provisions.[1]

In order to pray effectively, you need to pray the Word of God, which is His will.

Now this is the confidence that we have in Him, that if we ask anything according to His will, He hears us, And if we know that He hears us, whatever we ask, we know that we have the petitions that we have asked of Him (1 John 5:14 -15). This means that if you will study to know God's Word and His will for marriage and then pray, you will have that for which you have petitioned God. You can have your marriage stabilized, healed, fortified against attack, sanctified, blessed, favored, envied, and admired by the world you touch.

Everything God has promised in His Word is yours through faith and asking, believing that you receive when you pray. *Therefore I say to you, whatever things you ask when you pray, believe that you receive them, and you will have them* (Mark 11:24),

The challenge of life and marriage is to have faith in what God has promised in His word concerning Jesus Christ and the resulting abundant life.

4.
Marriage: A Gift From God

(or Whose Idea Was This Anyway?)

Jesus stated in Matt. 22:37, *You shall love the Lord your God with all your heart, with all your soul, and with all your mind.* This obviously is talking about our relationship with God. He desires to be first, to have the preeminence in our lives; he desires for us to be committed to Him.

God always uses marriage as an example of our relationship to Him. He even calls the Church the Bride of Christ. Many times, He has referred to Israel as adulterers when they worshipped other gods.

Marriage was created by God. When He recognized that Adam was alone, He created Eve to bless him with the gift of companionship and partnership. She became "bone of his bone" and "flesh of his flesh." Gen. 2:24 reads, *Therefore shall a man leave his father and his mother, and shall cleave unto his wife: and they shall be one flesh* (KJV). That word "cleave" means to be joined to, adhere, cling to, to catch by pursuit. Plainly stated, God wants you to be committed, hooked-up together without looking for an escape route. Isn't that just what He wants in a relationship with us. God is not looking for a way out. Every day He blesses us and gives us opportunities to receive His great love, because He is committed to us.

When you accept Jesus as Savior, you become one with the Father. Rather than it being just a statement of fact, it is something He wants you to actually experience on a spiritual level. In the same manner, He wants you to experience a physical and emotional oneness in your relationship with your spouse, causing you to be committed to one another, preferring one another over all others.[1] That is what God desires in your relationship with Him, and He wants that for your marriage.

Let's talk about this "oneness." Why is this so important, and how can it be a blessing? When you understand oneness, you begin to realize that what you do affects your spouse and vice versa. If you see yourselves as one, then you will begin to treat your partner differently. You will begin to want to do what benefits the other, and you will see that what benefits your spouse benefits you.

God did not send Jesus to die for us because it benefited Him. *We* were in need, so He not only gave us what *we* needed, He gave us His best in Jesus Christ. In return, we bless Him by giving Him praise, thanksgiving, obedience, and hopefully, our best.

Just what did God do for us?

If we don't get any other point across to our readers, there is one thing that we want you to fully understand: **God wants your marriage to reflect what He does for us.** He wants you to do for each other what He does for us. Well, what does He do? When we accept Jesus as Savior, a very unique thing happens. Our sins are forgiven, our slate is wiped clean, and our past is no longer remembered or held against us by God. He made the choice to do that. He also does not require us to be perfect for Him to love us – He loves as though we already are. He blesses us, not because we do things correctly all the time, but because He chooses to.

The cornerstone of our message is Jesus and His example. If you believe that Jesus is Lord and Savior of your life, the only marriage manual that's truly valid is God's Word. As you see in the Word what God's vision for marriage is, you have to desire it and believe that He can bring it to pass in your own situation.

How does God intend for marriage to be a blessing? Everything in our lives center around our relationship with God, and our lives should model that. Our families are a microcosm or a tiny example of what our relationship to God ought to be. The gift that He gave us through His Son is immeasurable. It needs to be your desire to give that same gift to your spouse. In order to do it, however, you must fully understand what the gift truly is.

What is God's Vision for Your Marriage?

Do you know God's vision for your marriage? God's vision for your marriage has eternal significance that can move you from the realm of impossibilities to the realm of possibilities.[2] If you can grasp hold of God's vision for your marriage, He is willing to empower you to do what is necessary to bring your home into agreement with His Word. It is, however, a matter of your faith. Everything you receive from God is a matter of faith: healing, deliverance, prosperity, and a successful marriage. And you need to allow everything you say and do to be birthed by your understanding of God's vision of marriage.[3]

Genesis 1:28 tells us, *And God blessed them, and God said unto them, Be fruitful, and multiply, and replenish the earth, and subdue it…(KJV)*.

God envisioned that we would prosper and our seed and our seed's seed would inherit both natural and spiritual blessings.[4] God desired, and still desires, for us to produce godly seed who honors and adores Him. His Word says that He blessed Adam and Eve.

Genesis 2:18 declares, *And the Lord God said, "It is not good for the man to be alone. I will make a companion who will help him"* (NLT). When we look closely at Scripture, we see that God, Himself, was the Creator of marriage; not a man, not a woman. God did it. Whose idea was this, anyway? God, the Father's! He determined that it was not good for man to be alone. It appears that sometimes men think women made up the concept of marriage so they would have someone to take care of them. It also seems that women think men must have invented it to have someone to cook and clean for them. The stark truth is that God is the One who had the vision of marriage and made it a reality. However, He also had specific ways He intended marriage to work. Unfortunately, with the progression of sin and time, marriage has taken on a whole new face of ungodliness.

God's vision for marriage was that it was to be a blessing, not a test or trial, or other obstacle put in your way to see if you get to go to Heaven; but a blessing.[5] Interestingly enough, God had a wonderful relationship with Adam, yet He saw a need for something more in him. Obviously, God would never give you something that would take away from your relationship with Him, so the conclusion to be drawn here is that God intended marriage to help you serve Him even better. If you can become fully aware of that, then you can go to the Father and say, "My marriage is not helping me serve you better, Lord. In fact, it's doing just the opposite. Help us to have the marriage You envisioned for us. Let Your vision be our vision." You need to desire the kind of relationship with your spouse that draws you closer to God. That is God's plan. God wants to prosper you, and He wants to do it through your marriage.

Understand that God wants a one-on-one, personal relationship with you. That comes first. It's during this personal time with the Father that you receive instructions in how to navigate this life. It's here where you hear the Father's heart on how He wants you to live and interact with others. That main "other" is your mate. Without that intimate time with God, you won't know how to treat each other.

If your marriage is failing, and you both *do* spend quality, private time with God; we could almost guarantee that someone in the relationship is walking in disobedience. Why? Because God will always refer you back to our mate. No matter how much we love God and want to serve Him, if you are not treating your spouse well, God will correct you. Whether you obey Him is another story. Let's look at a familiar triangle:

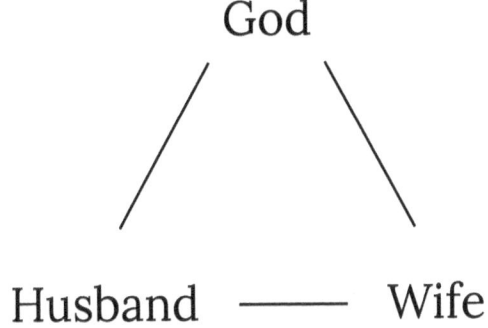

God is at the apex of the triangle; husband and wife are at the base. God has commanded in His word that we place no other gods before Him. The other gods of your life can be other people, things, aspirations or dreams. The beauty of all of God's plans for is that they are complete; so as you worship and adore God and desire to please Him in every way, you find in His word that He commands husbands to love their wives as Christ loves the Church and for wives to honor or respect their husbands (Ephesians 5:25-33).

What you discover is this: The only way for a couple to please God is to be a blessing to each other. Giving God first place in your individual life provides the motivation and direction to meet your spouse's needs and desires.

This is the basis of saying that as a couple, you give 100 percent and 100 percent to make the relationship prosper. That 100 percent is not given to your spouse directly, per se, but to God in obedience to His direction to love and honor one another. If you would dare to trust God enough to fully commit to His plan for marriage and your entire life, your life and marriage would be the blessing God has always intended it to be. When you understand that your conduct should be controlled by your relationship to God versus how your spouse is responding at the moment, it will change your marriage into a situation where God is committed to bringing success and blessings.

It must be reiterated that God created marriage to be a blessing, not only for you and your seed, but your seed's seed. In Malachi 2:15, the writer tells us that God sought a "godly seed." Our earnest prayer is that as long as time exists, our family line will be godly; that our children, grandchildren, and all other children to follow, until time ends, will pursue and serve the Lord with all their hearts. When God told Adam and Eve to be fruitful and multiply, that was His intention: that Adam's household would prosper and that all the generations that followed would be lovers of God. Obviously, that didn't happen because of the prevalence of sin in the earth. But thank God that He had a plan even for that! Through Jesus, we are still able to achieve God's vision. *Your* family could be the start of that godly line.

So, what happens when you see your marriage isn't becoming what God intended? Do you throw up your hands and say, "I guess it just wasn't meant to be."? NO, NO, a thousand times, NO! That's what they say in movies and on television. Don't live your life according to the dictates of this world system. Live it by the Word of God.

Your future will be anchored in God's power to enable you to flourish, multiply, walk in authority, and take control of the circumstances around you. Remember, further in Genesis 1:28, God told them to not only be fruitful and multiply, but that they would have dominion and subdue the earth. That simply means that you, as God's people, have the ability to take hold of your circumstances and change the things that need to be changed in your relationship; and to not be satisfied until you have God's best for your marriage. And it does take work! You must be willing to chase after God's vision for your marriage.

Look at Habakkuk 2:2-3: *Then the Lord answered me and said: "Write the vision And make it plain on tablets, That he may run who reads it. For the vision is yet for an appointed time; But at the end it will speak, and it will not lie. Though it tarries, wait for it; Because it will surely come, It will not tarry.* We would encourage you, as

God begins to unfold His vision for your marriage, to write it down and review it from time to time. The basic framework for marriage is written throughout the Word of God, but every couple is different. God has specific plans for your marriage, so He must be sought to discover the particulars. It must be a diligent quest, done with much prayer.

Begin to confess what Paul penned in 2 Corinthians 2:14, *Now thanks be to God who always leads us in triumph in Christ, and through us diffuses the fragrance of His knowledge in every place.* You can believe God to always cause you to triumph and be victorious in your pursuit of His will for your life; and when He has made you victors, will make known the fragrance of a life committed to God's plan everywhere you go.

Discover God's vision for your marriage. Pursue it, embrace it, and live expectantly, waiting for Him to bring it to pass.

5.
The Two Marriage Killers

The two most difficult things to get past in marriage are our innate selfishness and pride. If those two things could be checked at the door on our wedding day, and from now on, we would cut down on our conflicts by *at least* ninety-nine percent. Proverbs 13:10 clearly states, *Only by pride comes contention.* The NLT tells us that, *Pride leads to arguments.* We're totally convinced of that!

Think about the last argument or disagreement you had with your spouse. If you are honest about it, you will recognize that it was the result of your selfishness or pride. Pride is one of those things that arises in us to cause us to try to protect ourselves. The thought (whether conscious or unconscious) is, "How dare they do that to me or speak that way to me. Don't they know who I am? I'm somebody important." Pride convinces us that we should be treated a certain way.

The first thing we want to do is identify the two different kinds of pride. There is good or acceptable pride and there is improper pride, the kind that displeases God. Acceptable pride is pleasure or satisfaction taken in an achievement, possession, or association. A synonym would be self-respect. You can be proud of your children, proud of their accomplishments, or achievements. Where you develop a problem, though, is when you start to think your children are better than anyone else's. That's where improper or inappropriate pride enters.

The pride that God is against is arrogant, disdainful conduct, or haughtiness; an excessively high opinion of one's self. Simply put, pride is thinking more of yourself than you have the right to. Romans 12:3 says, *For I say...to everyone...not to think more highly of himself than he ought to think.* The NLT states, *As God's messenger, I give each of you this warning: Be honest in your estimate of yourselves.* You need to see yourselves as God sees you: redeemed people who are only that way because of Jesus.

Why does God hate pride? Because it allows you to take credit for things you had nothing to do with. Take, for example, the race or ethnicity you happen to be born. You had absolutely nothing to do with that. God is the one Who decided that. Therefore, you have no right to be proud of that. You certainly should not be sorry or disappointed with the race you are, but you can't be proud of it because **you did not do it.**

Look at pride from God's perspective. Proverbs 6:16-19 reads, *There are six things the Lord hates – no, seven things he detests: <u>haughty eyes</u>, a lying tongue, hands that kill the innocent, a heart that plots evil, feet that race to do wrong, a false witness who pours out lies, a person who sows discord among brothers* (NLT). In dealing with the "haughty eyes," in particular, the King James Version calls this "a proud look." God doesn't like it; He hates it; He detests it, and you need to also see it that way. Now, take a look at Mark 7:20-23: *And then he added, It is the thought-life that defiles you. For from within, out of a person's heart, come evil thoughts, sexual immorality, theft, murder, adultery, greed, wickedness, deceit, eagerness for lustful pleasure, envy, slander, <u>pride</u>, and foolishness. All these vile things come from within; they are what defile you and make you unacceptable to God (NLT).* Isn't it interesting that Jesus includes pride amongst all the other sins mentioned? In other words, it's not something you can take lightly because God doesn't. God hates it, and when you see it in yourself, you need put yourself in check.

Pride is the thing that makes you act unmannerly toward your mate. It's what makes you vengeful in your actions and causes you to become competitive instead of supportive.

When you feel violated, it causes you to say and do things that hurt. It's what makes you feel strong or superior. Let's look, however, at God's perspective on this matter. He tells us in Proverbs 16:32: *He who is slow to anger is better than the mighty: and he who rules his spirit than he who takes a city.* Pride will build walls in your relationship that can only be breached through brokenness. Your marriage should be about promoting unity and oneness, not division and separation. In other words, laying pride aside is what makes you truly strong.

Selfishness is driven by pride. Selfishness tells you,

"It must go my way." Or "If I don't get what I want, I'm the loser." You need to come to the place where you want the success of your marriage more than being "right" or having it your way. When your focus is on the goal of unity and achievement of a specific task rather than self-affirmation, you can neutralize pride and experience success in your relationship. How many times have we all, in pride, declared that we were right in a situation only to find out that we are indeed, "dead right." You may find yourself right but only at the expense of the hurting of your spouse. Was it worth it? Remember, the thing that has to win here is the marriage and preserving the heart and welfare of the other person.

Well, what exactly is marriage? Here is the dictionary definition: "A social institution by which a man and a woman are legally united and establish a new family unit; an intimate union." United, unit, and union clearly explain that in marriage, a man and a woman no longer are two separate individuals but are now one. We live in a new-age world that teaches that when two people get married, they remain their individual selves. It is because of that thinking that you may find yourself acting selfishly. When you realize, however, that you are no longer two but one, you will begin to see that what you do affects your partner and vice versa. This is clearly expressed in Ephesians 5:28-31, *So husbands ought to love their wives as their own bodies; he who loves his wife loves himself. For no one ever hated his own flesh, but nourishes and cherishes it, just as the Lord does the church. For we are members of His body, of His flesh and of His bones.*

For this reason, a man shall leave his mother and father and be joined to his wife, and the two shall become one flesh. So, you see, it's not about you and me anymore; it's about *us*.

The Death of Me

Certainly, you're familiar with the phrase, "This _____ is going to be the death of me!" Well, truer words were never spoken in regards to marriage. In order to have success in marriage, you must recognize that you can no longer hold onto who you were as an individual before marriage. There is nothing in our current culture of "me, myself, and I" that promotes the concept of oneness.

When pride is removed and the promotion of "us" is given priority, you become more open to the ideas and concerns of your mates. It becomes more about achieving success together than whose idea or plan was executed. Removal of pride will allow "our" plan to be implemented so that "we" experience the victory of "us."

One day while we were just sitting around thinking, we came to the realization that because we have been married so long, we have been a part of a new unit longer than we were part of our parents' family. Doesn't it make sense that we would begin to take on some of each other's characteristics after being together for so many years? Certainly! We have been "us" longer than we've been individuals.

Remember we said that selfishness and pride are the two marriage killers. Those things disappear when you realize that it's not about protecting *my* rights and *my* feelings and *my* individuality; it's about protecting *our* marriage. It's about protecting *us;* doing the things that will bless "both of us."

Choosing Wisdom and Humility

Let's look at the negative side of pride and how it can and *will* affect our relationship with God and others. St. Augustine defined pride as "the love of one's own excellence". Thus, pride causes us to focus on what is right with us and unfortunately, what's wrong with others. Proverbs 13:10, according to the New International Version, instructs us that where there is strife, pride will be found, also. Each of us can attest to the fact that, in the majority of the situations where strife, envy, and disagreements have erupted, pride manifested in one or both parties involved in the dispute.

God hates pride because it causes those under its influence to forget, or not be able, to distinguish between the Creator and the created. Pride can cause us to become full of ourselves, arrogant, and self-seeking in our attitudes and actions. This behavior trait is not one that leads to peace and harmony with God or anyone else.

Our world is sometimes filled with opportunities to feel less than wonderful about our personal progress in life's journey. Some would advise that one should begin to assess and advertise their value and admitted successes, but let us ever remember that God is the source and Creator of our *everything*! We must learn to rejoice and have a sense of satisfaction in the care and love expressed in each individual by God, who loves us and is determined to have a love relationship with us. There is nothing wrong with acknowledging that we are wonderfully made and performing well, but give credit to the designer, maintainer, and constant enabler, God.

When we are able to see the hand of God working in others, then we might be willing to take some advice from them. Scripture declares that wisdom is found in those who take advice. For those of us who are married, that means God had a hand in the creation and development of our mate who should be held in high esteem. If you value and esteem your spouse, you will allow them the opportunity to provide input worthy of consideration and evaluation. Pride that causes you to devalue your spouse will result in strife in your home.

James 4:6 says, *But he gives us more grace. That is why Scripture says: "God opposes the proud but shows favor to the humble"* (NIV). Humility says, "I appreciate my Creator's part in the wonder of me." It's not that we are nothing; we are awesome demonstrations of the creative power and sustaining devotion of God.

When you find yourself focusing on what is right with you at the expense of comparison to or degradation of another, ask God to help you remove pride and worship the Creator and not the creation. God has promised grace and favor to the humble.

6.

Can Love Really Last Forever?

We've observed many wedding ceremonies, and are struck by many of the common things that occur. Nearly always, as the bride floats down the aisle to meet her groom, they are both filled with emotion, joy, and anticipation. Many times, there are tears.

The tears come, we believe, because they each begin to have an awareness of the gravity of what they are about to do. We're certain most of you experienced the same thing. At the moment of reciting your vows, you think you really mean what you are saying. Here is a typical vow:

> I, _____, take thee, _____ to be my wedded wife/husband, to have and to hold from this day forward, for better for worse, for richer for poorer, in sickness and in health, to love and to cherish, 'til death do us part, according to God's holy ordinance, and thereto I pledge thee my faith.

You put your whole heart into stating those promises; but somewhere along the way, you forget how you felt on your wedding day. You intended to love forever, but as time progresses, and in the face of life's challenges, you realize you don't really know how. How can you *possibly* stay in love forever? Conventional wisdom tells us that it's impossible to do. *But the wisdom that is from above is first pure, then peaceable, gentle, willing to yield, full of mercy and good fruits, without partiality and without hypocrisy.* (James 3:17).

Let's talk about this issue of love. Part of the problem that people experience is something they call "falling out of love." They can say that because they are basing their love on feelings. Well, there is a kind of love that God commands that has very little to do with feelings. It's called *agape*. It's unconditional love. The best definition we have come up with is: "Doing that which benefits the other person." Obviously, you cannot command feelings, but you can command actions. Agape (or the God-kind of love) is more about doing than feeling. It requires a clear determination of will and judgment.

In Ephesians 5:25, we read, *Husband, love your wives just as Christ also loved the church and <u>gave</u> Himself for her.* The love that Christ exhibited with His death on the cross was not a touchy, feely type of love. He knew that the only way to redeem us back to the Father was to allow Himself to be sacrificed for our sakes. Love was something He *did*, not *felt*. Therefore, Paul commands husbands to love their wives by <u>giving</u> their lives to them. Further, in Titus 2:3-4, Paul states, *the older women, likewise… that they admonish the young women to love their husbands.*

In other words, this love is the result of deliberately giving of yourself to meet the needs of another person.[1]

It requires action on the part of the lover. The only way such demands can be made is if you understand that the kind of love God wants you to operate in most of the time is the kind of love that never fails: the God-kind of love, agape. When you act lovingly, feelings generally follow.

Unfortunately, most of the time, when people say, "I've fallen out of love with you," what they really mean is, "You don't make me feel good anymore." It's that whole selfishness thing rearing its ugly head again. True love, genuine love, is not based on what you do for me, but what I do for you. Remember our definition: Doing that which benefits the other person. The God-kind of love causes me to look out for you, not myself. What am I doing to make you feel loved, accepted and secure? We don't discount the love that is derived from sharing, communicating, having common goals and purpose of heart, or even sexual attraction. A healthy marriage will experience the joy of friendship, the excitement of intimacy and the dedication of agape love.[2] It's the commanded love, however, that will sustain a marriage through every season and episode of life. When the feelings wane, God's love will continue to do all the mundane, day-to-day things like pay the bills, do the laundry, cook the meals, tend the children and show kindness.

This is a perfect segue into an important discussion on 1 Corinthians 13. You should really read the whole chapter, but for our purposes, we'll concentrate on verses 4-8 from the Amplified Bible:

Love endures long and is patient and kind; love never is envious nor boils over with jealousy; is not boastful or vainglorious, does not display itself haughtily. It is not conceited - arrogant and inflated with pride; it is not rude (unmannerly), and does not act unbecomingly. Love [God's love in us] does not insist on its own rights or its own way, for it is not self-seeking; it is not touchy or fretful or resentful; it takes no account of the evil done to it - pays no attention to a suffered wrong. It does not rejoice at injustice and unrighteousness, but rejoices when right and truth prevail. Love bears up under anything and everything that comes, is ever ready to believe the best of every person, its hopes are fadeless under all circumstances and it endures everything [without weakening]. Love never fails - never fades out or becomes obsolete or comes to an end.... Certainly, that Scripture sounds like a tall order, but God never tells you to do something without equipping you to do it. After reading this passage, you see clearly that indeed love *can* last forever if you are applying the right kind of love.

One of the couples we coached came to us expressing that they no longer had emotional feelings towards each other, but that they loved each other "in the Lord." We hear that from a lot of people, not just married couples. What they mean is that they have no emotional tie to that person; but because the Bible says we are to love, we say we love them "in the Lord." Following a reading of this Scripture, we asked the couple this question: "Now that you've read this, can you honestly say that you love each other even 'in the Lord'?"

They had to admit that based on the way they treated each other, perhaps they didn't.

It's very true that the ooey-gooey feelings of romantic love can disappear, but they can be recaptured simply by applying the God-kind of love.

Keep in mind that it is necessary to demonstrate the acts of love that cause your spouse to feel loved. Gary Chapman's book, *The Five Love Languages*, elaborates on this point and describes five basic ways that people interpret love: Acts of Service, Quality Time, Physical Touch, Words of Affirmation, and Gifts.[3] The author points out, for instance, that although you may feel love by receiving gifts like flowers and cards; your mate may feel love when you perform acts of service like folding the laundry. In other words, if love to your mate means physical touch, then the way you show love to that person is to touch them. Therefore, it is vitally important to do loving acts in response to your partner's love language. Doing those things will cause a response of appreciation on the part of your mate that will, in turn, cause you to desire to do more things; and before you know it, you're chasing each other around the house again!

The Risk of Unconditional Love

Have you noticed how much easier it is to love someone who loves you in return? Of course, you have; it's what we expect. Unfortunately, there are times when our acts of love and kindness are not reciprocated. Now what?

The solution to this dilemma is really quite simple (yes, simple, not easy) when we look at God's Word. Romans 5:8 tells us, *This is real love. It is not that we loved God, but that he loved us and sent his Son as a sacrifice to take away our sins. Dear friends, since God loved us that much, we surely ought to love each other* (NLT). This is what loving unconditionally is all about. Again, the definition of agape, the God-kind of love, is doing what benefits the other. This is the kind of love this passage of Scripture is speaking of. In other words, it doesn't matter so much what your spouse does or doesn't do, you must still choose to love. And there are risks involved.

The risk we take when we choose to love unconditionally is rejection. That is the risk God took when, while we were still in our sin, Jesus died for us. Being the omniscient One He is, He knew that many would reject His love. That, however, did not stop Him. He was still willing to take the risk.

Remember, God did not wait until we were perfect before He gave us His greatest sacrifice. He loved us as though we already were! As challenging as that sounds, He wants us to do the same. Trust me, this cannot be done in our own human power; it requires the power of God.

When you choose to do things God's way and love unconditionally, He blesses your obedience. Scripture teaches us that to know God is to love Him, and to love God is to obey Him.

Take the risk. Show the love. It will reap great rewards. You may not see all of them immediately; but if you are faithful to obey, God's promise is sure.

A New Determination

Regarding those vows you took, here is the good news: Not only does God expect us to deliver on our promises, He supplies the power to do it; so absolutely, without God providing the strength for us to keep our word, most marriages are doomed to be short lived.

A forever marriage is not a fantasy. It can be attained by a great deal of hard work and determination and with our eyes fixed on Father God for direction, strength and wisdom. We do have to ask Him for it, and He will give it to us liberally and won't make us feel ashamed for asking. Some Scriptures to keep in mind and add to your spiritual arsenal:

Philippians 4:13, *For I can do everything with the help of Christ who gives me the strength I need (NLT).*

James 1:5, *If you need wisdom -- if you want to know what God wants you to do -- ask him, and he will gladly tell you. He will not resent your asking (NLT).*

I Corinthians 13:7, *[Love] always looks for the best, never looks back, but keeps going to the end (Message).*

7.
Being Best Friends

Think back to when you were growing up and you designated someone as your best friend. Why did you bestow such an honor on that person? What qualities did they exhibit that caused you to think of them differently from all your other friends or acquaintances? They were probably someone who demonstrated loyalty; listened to you when you spoke; made you feel important; validated your ideas; shared honest feelings and shared similar interests. When everyone else might have abandoned you, they probably made you feel that they would stick closely to your side. Your best friend assured you that whatever you shared with them, no matter how bizarre or weird, would go no further than the two of you. You trusted your best friend. You spent more time with that person than anyone else.

In a large portion of the couples we have coached over the years, one common factor was present: They were either no longer best friends or never were to begin with. Someone else or something else had taken that esteemed spot.

God never intended for a man and woman to simply occupy the same house. Marriage was never intended to be a way in which two people share bills and have legal sex; and in the process, maybe bring a couple of children on the scene. The dictionary describes that as a "marriage of convenience."

As we've stated, marriage is a gift from God. We dedicated a whole chapter to understanding this gift, but let's just say that part of that gift is recognizing that one of the greatest gifts *within* the gift is having an in-house best friend.

Being best friends requires spending time together - on purpose. Here comes the work. If you're used to spending additional hours at work or with other people, you are going to have to make a quality decision to make an adjustment in your thinking and your actions. You'll have to say "no" to some of those extra activities that exclude your spouse.

One important aspect of being together is learning to do it alone.[1] That sounds a bit like an oxymoron, but you'd be surprised how many couples say they spend time together when, in actuality, there is always someone else around - children, other couples, television, etc. Sometimes just the thought of spending time alone with your partner is frightening if you haven't done it in a while. One husband once told us that he shudders at the idea of being alone with his wife because he's afraid he won't have anything to say to her. *Tragic!* That may very well be the case for you, but you have to start somewhere. It's very easy to crowd so many other things into your life that you no longer have time for each other; and if you're not careful, you will do everything possible to avoid spending time together because it's what has become comfortable. Here is something of a test question for you. If you had to spend an entire month together with no other human contact, could you do it and still remain sane? *Selah!* (Pause and think about this.)

How can we break this cycle? You need to make an intentional decision to set aside time for each other. Remember, we said that it would require an adjustment in your thinking. In other words, you're now going to have to set new priorities, and stick to them. In some cases, you will have to go back and do the things that attracted you to each other in the first place. In Rev. 2:4-5, Jesus says, *I have this against you, that you have left your first love. Remember, therefore from where you have fallen; repent and do the first works...* Now, obviously Christ was speaking to the Church in regard to our love for God, but it can easily be applied to your love for your marriage partner because the principle is the same. You've heard it over and over again that what you did to fall in love, you must do to stay in love. And the "what" may be different for every couple, but there are some similar, practical things that most couples can do to revive the friendship:

Decide together on a day and time once a week to have a date.

Set it in stone. This may require you to find a baby sitter, but it doesn't have to be something expensive. You would be surprised how just going to a little café for coffee and dessert can do wonders. We have made some of our most life-changing decisions over coffee and pie. Thank God for Baker's Square! Granted, it will take a major commitment on your part, and it may be a bit awkward, at first. You may find yourself struggling through long periods of silence.

Use this time to get re-acquainted. Keep it light. This is not the appropriate time to discuss tough issues. Start by simply talking about how you spent your day. As you get more and more comfortable, you will be amazed how you will begin to share your heart with each other – your hopes, your dreams. It's when you get into each other's hearts that you really know what the other is all about.

Have devotions and prayer together.

Again, this should be something that is light-hearted. There are numerous devotional books at any bookstore, or you can simply read a Proverb together every day. In fact, we have included one at the end of this book for your convenience, and to help you get started. Afterwards, you might pray a short prayer for God to bless your day. (This would not be the suitable time to call down fire from Heaven.) We have had couples tell us that they feel weird praying in front of each other. Please remember that this is not a time to worry about being critiqued for your skill in praying. It's just another way to hear each other's heart reach out to God.

Re-learn the art of touching.

We're not necessarily talking about sexual touching. Remember when you were dating and how you always found yourselves touching in some form or another. You held hands or you lay your heads on each other's shoulders or laps. You managed to find some way to be in close physical contact with the other. Because you're pulled in so many directions, sometimes, you may have forgotten the joy of touching and being close. Make a point to sit closely to one another while watching television. Allow your upper arms or legs to touch. Hold hands.

Be Consistent.

Continue doing all the little things you used to do and incorporate some new ones. Wake up each morning with the thought, "What special way can I let my partner know I care." Remember when you were dating and tried to do everything possible to impress each other? Don't let that stop. There should be no time in the relationship where you just coast. In other words, don't take each other for granted.

Be protective of each other.

Don't allow others to speak negatively about your spouse. Don't correct each other in public or show negative body language, such as rolling eyes or heavy sighs. NEVER expose your mate's shortcomings to others. Rather, discipline yourself only to speak of his/her positive qualities.

Ladies, you MUST learn to honor your husbands.

If you've ever wanted the key to your husband's heart, it's necessary to understand why honor is so important to him. The fact is, that is how God created him. God created us in His image, and one of the ways you demonstrate your love to Him is through praise. Your husband is the same. Look at Ephesians 5:33: *Nevertheless let each one of you in particular so love his wife as himself; and let the wife see that she respects her husband.* For even more clarity, let's read the Amplified Bible for that same verse: *However, let each man of you (without exception) love his wife as (being in a sense) his own self; and let the wife see that she respects and reverences her husband - that she notices him, regards him, honors him, prefers him, venerates and esteems him; and that she defers to him, praises him, and loves and admires him exceedingly.* That's about as clear as a bell! Men respond to praise and admiration. It prompts them to do even more to continue to receive that praise. Of course, women respond to it as well, but not nearly the same way men do.

Some of you are still waiting for greatness to come out of your husbands. Guess what? You are the vehicle through which it will be brought out.

"Behind every great man is an admiring wife." Your husband needs you to be proud of him. He needs to know that you think the world of him; that if nobody else thinks well of him, his wife does. Your husband needs to know that when he walks across that threshold into his house, he is the most important person on the face of the earth.

The irony of this is that women tend to be more critical of their husbands than complimentary. They have been somehow convinced that criticism is what will motivate change. Just the opposite is true. Criticism causes your husband to be defensive. and rebellious. It will give him reasons to find other things to do than spend time with you. Who wants to be around someone who constantly makes them feel bad about themselves? Admiration, on the other hand, causes him to be energized; it motivates him to do better. God did not bring us to Himself through devaluation. Instead, *therefore with lovingkindness have I drawn you* (Jeremiah. 31:3). Remember, our goal in this book is to encourage you to be like Christ in your relationship with each other.

Simply said, men thrive on admiration. Therefore, ladies, if you want to see your husband succeed; if you want to see your marriage flourish; if you want to have your husband do the little (and big) things you desire from him, lavish him with honor, praise, and admiration. We promise, you will be astonished at the results! We know some of you may be saying to yourselves that your husband has no redeemable qualities worth praising. By all means, don't lie, but you need to go back to when you first met him and remember the things that drew you to him. We guarantee they are not all gone. There is still something left for you to admire about your husband. Even if it is simply that you appreciate how he goes out every day to work and supports the family. Verbalize it, and make him feel like he can go out and conquer the world because every man wants to feel that way. Just start by noticing the small things and work up to the bigger ones, but make a huge deal of the small ones. The more you praise, the more he'll give you reason to do so.

Here's a little something worth tucking under your hat as you consider ways to honor and admire your husband. Men are most attracted to people who make them feel good about themselves. Many times, when a man becomes unfaithful to his wife, it's not because he's found someone prettier or someone with a shapelier body than his wife. It's usually because there is a Miss Thing somewhere who thinks the world of him, and doesn't hesitate to let him know it. *She* finds no fault with him. *She* thinks he is perfect. *She* thinks he walks on water. *She* is the one he wants to spend time with if all he gets when he's home is nagging and criticism. On the other hand, being a champion of your husband and profusely bestowing praise on him, makes him less susceptible to other women's admiration. **You** need to be his most enthusiastic fan.

Men your wife NEEDS you to see her as precious.

She needs to feel that you think that she is the most beautiful woman in the world. Of course, she knows in her heart that she isn't, but she wants to feel like she is, at least, to you. When she feels beautiful, she feels sexy. When she feels sexy, you'll feel desired because she will want to experience closeness with you. You are the one responsible for making her feel that way.

Your wife needs to not only *know* that you love her; she needs to hear it, often. She needs you to be understanding and not think of her as just another "typical woman" when she's feeling emotional or hurt. She needs compassion and empathy. She also needs for you to be a good listener and not be distracted by the "butterflies" that flit about as she is speaking to you.

Begin to declare her as a virtuous woman, whose "price is far above rubies" (Proverbs 31:10, KJV). Sometimes, just the acknowledgement of her contributions and hard work is all that is needed. Demonstrate your appreciation and affection for her by trusting her enough to share your thoughts. Let her know you believe she will protect your inner feelings from all outside invaders.

Continue to be polite to each other.

Words like "please" and "thank you" never go out of style. It is surprising how many couples, after being married for a time, lose those little courtesies they once had for each other. Of course, they would never neglect such things with strangers or on their jobs.

In your marriages, make it your goal to allow familiarity to breed love, appreciation, respect, loyalty, adoration, and praise – not contempt.

The "Mommy" Factor

We're still on the subject of being best friends, but there's an important issue we would be remiss not to discuss. This area is particularly pertinent to women with children.

In an attempt to spend more time with your husband, it's necessary to understand the changing roles of women. When you first marry, your husband is generally the center of your attention; and that's just how he likes it. And he doesn't expect that to ever change. Then you decide together to start a family. You both get excited. While you're pregnant, the baby isn't truly a reality, yet, but you both have great expectations and anticipation. Finally, the baby arrives, and you bring her home. Now, it's *very* real.

You soon come to realize, Mom, that you now have another little person vying for your time and attention. Unfortunately, because she's so helpless, you can't just ignore her needs. At the same time, your husband is also in need of your attention. At this point you feel torn, but you know that you cannot say to your young baby, "Sorry, Precious. Mommy can't take care of you right now. Daddy needs me."

Your husband is pulling on one side and your child on the other. What do you do? Well, most mothers make the unconscious decision that because your husband is the adult, he'll understand if you give all your devotion to your child right now because she's *so* needy. The problem is, children are always needy. So, weeks turn into months, months turn into years, and your husband gets the very strong message that he is no longer number one. He would be too embarrassed to tell you that he is jealous of his child. And in some cases, he may even begin to resent the child; but mostly, he resents his wife. The result: you stop communicating, you cease being lovers (there's no time), and you cease being friends. Eventually, the children leave home, and all that's left are two strangers who simply live in the same house together. Here is a scary fact: The divorce rate among empty nesters is extraordinarily high! Any guesses why?

How do we prevent this from happening?

First, establish in your mind that your role as the doting, attentive mother is a temporary one. Remember, children normally are not permanent residents of your home, and they will not always need you at their beck and call.

Next, learn to put your children to bed early!! Sometimes when we share that suggestion with couples, especially wives, we get a reaction similar to if we'd just asked them to plan a trip to the moon every weekend. In other words, that seems almost impossible. Usually, the first excuse we hear is, "But when will Dad get a chance to spend time with the kids?" We promise that with a little planning and communicating this can be accomplished. Here's one idea: Use dinnertime as a bonding time, and have Dad be the bedtime storyteller. Whatever method you decide to use, make it a priority. Believe me, Mom, you need the break, and your relationship needs the time. Establish together what that early bedtime should be, but you want, at least, two hours of alone time before your own bedtime.

Finally, understand that your role as an attentive wife, lover, and friend is until "death do us part." Your husband needs to feel attended to. He needs to feel that he matters, that you place him as a high priority.

Husbands, you are not off the hook here. It's important for you to help your wife to keep you high on her list. Here are some things *you* can do:

- Be understanding and reasonable. Your wife is doing the best she can in trying to juggle motherhood and "wifedom." Despite her efforts, she sometimes feels like she's a failure at both. Trying to please everyone is exhausting!

- Praise her efforts and make her feel valued as a person

- Help pick up around the house. Identify some of the activities she really doesn't like to do, and give her a hand.

- Allow her some "me" time. When a woman has even a little bit of time to pamper herself, it does wonders for her state of mind.

- Take your wife to dinner occasionally or *you* cook.

- Remember that weekly date.

- Father your children. In other words, *you* take the lead role as caregiver sometimes to give your wife a break. Some may call this baby sitting, but you are merely fathering.

It is vitally important that couples see each other as best friends. There should be no one you trust more than your mate. That's how God intended it to be, and there's no greater joy. No one else should know you as well as your spouse. If, however, you do not nurture that closeness, it will fade and eventually become invisible.

8.
Dispelling the Myths

There are several misconceptions that people have about marriage that we want to take a moment to dismantle:

Marriage is a 50/50 proposition.

When people make that statement, they are basically saying that they will do their part if the other person does his/her part. However, God expects you to do your part 100 percent of the time and to the best of your ability with His help. It's not about comparing yourself to how your partner performs, but how you personally perform according to God's Word. God's Word is your measuring stick, not your mate. When you give your all to obeying and following God's plan, you will bless our mate and open the door for God to faithfully bless you and your marriage.

Marriage is a test

As we have stated earlier, God created marriage to be a blessing, designed to enhance our lives and service to God. It is to be a place where two people can grow and help each other draw closer to God. God said that it was not good for man to be alone and that is why He created woman. They are to cleave or adhere firmly and loyally to each other until death separates them. Marriage was meant to be a little bit of Heaven on earth – not a test of survival skills.

All you need is love

This one will depend upon the type of love you have. Agape, or unconditional love, is the kind of love that keeps a marriage together; but even that must be mixed with faith. Love based on feelings only lasts momentarily because feelings change so often. Unconditional love, God's love, will stay the course and stand the test of time. This God-type of love can only be received through a personal relationship with Jesus Christ. Unfortunately, we can only give what we, ourselves, have received.

"I love him/her; I'm just not *in love* with him/her."

This one, obviously, goes right along with the previous one. As stated before, when people say that, they generally mean they don't feel the same way they used to. Feelings are unpredictable, and any marriage based solely on feelings is doomed right from the start. In the chapter entitled, "Can Love Really Last Forever?" we answered that question with a loud and profound, "YES," because the love we refer to is unconditional love.

"We have just grown apart."

The reality here is that you have lost the desire to continue to get to know, and accept your spouse and are only concentrating on your own needs and perspective. You must continue to pursue your initial aspiration to know and understand your partner because he/she is constantly growing and changing, as are you. What you thought you knew about your mate last year may be different this year because he/she has grown in knowledge, experience, and wisdom. The older we get, the more we see the world through different eyes. It's necessary to keep your eyes on each other as you progress in your marriage and life. Stay current with the changes that take place in each other with wonder and gratefulness. Appreciate the gift that God has given you in your spouse. Remember, it's about your mate's needs rather than your own.

"If I don't watch out for me, who will?"

We have a hard time with not putting ourselves first because we don't really trust that, if we focus on our mate's needs, our needs will, indeed, be met. So, we think it's important to take care of #1. Of course, you should not neglect yourself, by any means, but **YOU** cannot be your main purpose or focus.

If you are trusting in your mate to meet your needs, you may very well be disappointed; yet you are also not to put your trust in yourself, either. We are to trust God. He is the One who will make sure we are well taken care of. The care and consideration we give to our spouse may not be reciprocated, but that does not give us license to stop doing it. Either we are going to trust God or not. He is faithful! And He will prove it if we give Him the opportunity.

To love your mate with the God-kind of love is to seek to meet his/her needs. If you believe this is God's plan and desire for your marriage, then God is the one looking out for you. As you obey God's directive to love unselfishly, He will bless you far better than you can in your strength and schemes. Allow your personal relationship with God to bring you peace, joy, and fulfillment.

"My home is my castle and where I rule."

If nowhere else on earth, your home should be where God rules. Your home and relationship with your family is not a "God-free zone." It is not where you let it all hang out but where you learn to allow God to have complete control in the shelter of loved ones. This is the place to make your best attempt to get it right, and when you blow it, be forgiven by those who love you and know your heart. Home is where you rehearse God's plan before you go on the road with your testimony. Seek God's presence in your life and home. Desire to be His representative wherever you are may go, especially home.

9.
The Dreaded "F" Word

Many of you may hold onto another old myth that says time heals all wounds. The truth is that only God's love and His wisdom can bring about true healing to our situations.[1] Procrastination or time will not help. You have to allow God to work on the inside of you in such a way that brings about repentance and forgiveness.

Why are those things important in a marriage? Because left unattended, offenses can cause severe damage to a relationship. We're reminded of one of the stories in the "Three Stooges" series about Niagara Falls. Apparently, a traumatic event occurred having to do with Niagara Falls; and every time that name is mentioned, "Moe" would go into a deep trance and remember that event. The result was that he wants to kill someone. He would be fine and go along his merry way, seemingly, normal (or at least as normal as a Stooge could be) until that phrase was mentioned. Then all of a sudden, his whole countenance changed, and unpleasant things began to happen. You may be that way when it comes to thinking that time heals. All someone needs to do is bring up the subject, and you're hot on it again. You're mad all over again. There's no resolution. Time does not heal. The person who hurt you may die, but when someone brings them to mind, you'll be mad and angry all over again about what you perceive he/she did to you.

Many things don't pass away with time. They simply go sub-surface and manifest themselves in other places and ways. Facing your predicaments and challenges and turning them over to God is the only solution to getting healed from them. God will bring a resolution to your situations if you allow Him to.

When unpleasant situations arise, you need to ask yourself, "What is God's best here, and how can I surrender my will and feelings over to the plan and direction of God for our lives?"[2] First John 1:7-9 states, *But if we walk in the light, as He is in the light, we have fellowship with one another, and the Blood of Jesus Christ his Son cleanses us from all sin. If we say that we have no sin, we deceive ourselves, and the truth is not in us. If we confess our sins, he is faithful and just to forgive us our sins, and cleanse us from all unrighteousness.* Just as you know when you sin against God and need to ask for forgiveness, you know when you have hurt your mate.[3] You may not know how deeply; but based on the response you received or the iciness of the atmosphere you're experiencing, you know you just did or said the wrong thing. And to say that you don't, you're not being honest. So, if you know it, and your desire is to have God's vision for your life and your marriage, why not repent and ask for forgiveness? Immediately! Right away! Now! Instantly! Apologize to that mate because your ultimate desire is to maintain the relationship and bless your mate. You ask God for forgiveness; you ought to be able to do it with your mate. You should be able to admit your mistakes or misdeed to anyone if you don't have pride or selfishness ruling you. When you recognize that you've missed it, you need to repent and seek forgiveness.

Let's delve more deeply into this idea of repentance. James 5:16 says, *Confess your trespasses to one another, and pray for one another, that you may be healed. The effective, fervent prayer of a righteous man avails much.* So, you need to be sorry for the wrong attitudes and actions you have committed. It's possible that sometimes you don't want to confess it because you're enjoying the result of your "misstep", but remember that, just as with your relationship with God, sin only has pleasure for a season. You should be able to look down the road and see what it's going to cost you. It's going to cause you a problem if you don't get it right by asking for forgiveness as soon as possible. And if you believe in the vision God has for your marriage, then you'll find yourself trying to resolve the situation, recognizing that it's worth the trouble or discomfort you may experience in the process. You need to see the end of it; that if it's not corrected, no genuine good can come of it. It's important to turn away from (repent) and repair whatever you have done to hurt your spouse. Abandon the offending deed because you recognize that you don't want to hurt your mate; you do not want to cause conflict in your home as a result of something you've done that is not right. Pursuing forgiveness from the offended party allows the wound to be cleansed and the healing process to begin.

The Scripture above also says to pray for one another. Praying for each other (and with each other) is one of the best ways to tear down walls that may have been erected. When you pray together, you are able to hear each other's hearts as they are poured out to God. You'll get a better understanding of how the other one thinks and is processing life. You're present to hear his/her desires, concerns, visions, and plans for you. You are able to hear what each other is asking God to do in the relationship. Sometimes you hear things you didn't know: the hurts you didn't know were there that you can fix because you want to bring healing. You want to help. You want to bring wholeness to your mate.

The healing the verse talks about is forgiveness. It's critical that you do not give the seeds of hurt a chance to take root and grow.[4] Many of you could think back to times when your spouse hurt you, and it took months, maybe years, for them to repent or apologize. By the time he/she got around to getting it straight, the wound was deep and sometimes crippling. You may have eventually resolved it, but what great pain you suffered in the meantime. As with your relationship to God; when you miss it, repentance must come quickly as the consequences of delay could be devastating. You don't want to do anything that will shut off the full flow of God's blessings from your life. Most of us have the attitude that we don't want to "mess with"

God, but somehow, we think that we can "mess with" our mate and get away with it. Again, this is the misconception that our homes are some kind of "God-free zone." However, God placed your spouse in your life to be a blessing to you, to be a representative of Him, in many cases, to minister to you, to care for you, to be His instrument of love in your life. Consequently, He will not allow you to treat your mate unkindly without negative results or repercussions.

When you've offended your spouse, your repentance and request for forgiveness must be specific and genuine. It's all too easy to simply say, "I'm sorry if you felt that I hurt you." That makes it sound like you think their hurt is their own personal problem, not that you genuinely care that they were hurt. You're not saying that you are sorry for causing pain but that you are sorry for them having a reaction to the pain. The difference is subtle, but there is a difference, nevertheless. Would you dare go to God and say, "God, I'm sorry you didn't like the sin I just committed. I know it's a personal problem you have. It's not a big deal to me, and I don't see anything wrong with it; but since I guess I offended you, I'm sorry." Of course not! And you shouldn't do it to your mate either.

If you care enough, you will get to the root of the pain and be honestly sorry for being the cause of it. You may, of course, need to educate your mate to the fact that it was simply a mistake and not at all intentional, but you need to be penitent just the same because you don't want a seed of bitterness to grow and affect other areas of your relationship that may come back and cause *you* pain when you least expect it. It will seem to come out of nowhere, but it will be the result of a seed you planted that was not dealt with soon enough.

There are negative consequences for procrastinating in repentance, and you need to avoid them. Of course, your relationship to your spouse differs in some ways from that with God. God knows your heart accurately and truly. Your spouse knows only what you say and do as a basis of your heart's content and intent.

Repentance and forgiveness are a two-sided coin. When you wrong your mate, you must repent, turn away from that thing and ask for and receive forgiveness. When, however, you are on the receiving end of the offense, you must be willing to forgive. There was a quote in a Readers' Digest quite some time ago that said, "Holding a grudge is like taking poison and waiting for the other person to die." Holding a grudge is a symptom of unforgiveness. Unforgiveness is a symptom of pride, and remember, God hates pride.

Another very critical thing that happens when you are slow in dealing with offenses in your marriage is that your prayers are hindered. I Peter 3:7 states, *Husbands, likewise, dwell with them with understanding, giving honor to the wife, as to the weaker vessel, and as being heirs together of the grace of life, that your prayers may not be hindered.* God is concerned about how you treat your spouse. Although this specific Scripture is targeting the husband, there are enough other verses that tell the wife how to treat her mate that you can easily conclude it works both ways. You cannot treat your mate shabbily and expect God to move on your behalf. If your prayers don't seem to be going any higher than the ceiling, or there seems to be a blockage between you and God; you need to conduct a little inventory in your home. Assess how you're treating each other; check-up on your love walk. It's serious business.

Forgiveness and repentance bring healing. Ephesians 4:26-27, 32 tells us, *Be angry, and do not sin": do not let the sun go down on your wrath, nor give place to the devil. And be kind to one another, tenderhearted, forgiving one another, just as God in Christ forgave you.* If you desire to be healed of hurts, you need to replace anger with forgiveness. Obviously, anger is a genuine emotion that you experience, but God's Word tells how to respond to that anger. When you let loose that anger, it can have dire consequences. God says not to sin when you become angry, but that you must not allow the sun to set upon your wrath or rage. In other words, you must not let it linger; you must deal with it quickly before it consumes you. You need to be determined to have a resolution. Although you may not literally resolve the offense in one day, you must commit to working toward a timely, peaceful ending.

As we've said before, this is serious business. Perhaps this next Scripture will convince you of the gravity of forgiveness. Matthew 6:14-15 says it this way: *If you forgive those who sin against you, your heavenly Father will forgive you. But if you refuse to forgive others, your Father will not forgive your sins (NLT)*. That means big trouble, folks. If God doesn't forgive you, you won't see His face. Can any of us afford to be lax in this area?

It seems easier, sometimes, doesn't it, to apply these words to everywhere else but homes? We often speak of our homes as our refuge, our castles, and the place where we can let our hair down. All those descriptions may be true, but remember your home should not be a place that excludes God. The instructions God gives for dealing with people is not just meant for the ones outside your walls. They absolutely apply to each member of your family. You can't just forgive the grocery clerk for speaking sharply to you this morning; you must do the same for your spouse.

You may be asking, "Well how many times am I supposed to forgive for that same thing he/she does over and over again? Peter asked the same question to Jesus in Matthew 19:21-22. Peter thought that seven times was a sufficient number of times to forgive. However, Jesus told him that it was more like seventy times seven. In other words, however many times that it is necessary is how many times you forgive. Matthew Henry, in his Commentary, explains it best: "It does not look well for us to keep count of the offenses done against us by our brethren. There is something of ill-nature in scoring up the injuries we forgive, as if we would allow ourselves to be revenged when the measure is full. It is necessary to pass by injuries, without reckoning how often; to forgive, and forget. God multiplies His pardons, and so should we. We should make it our constant practice to forgive injuries, and should accustom ourselves to it till it becomes habitual."[5]

Your wheels are probably turning and some of you out there saying, "I might forgive, but I'll *never* forget. How could I possibly?" Perhaps a workable definition will help you understand how it is possible. Forgiving someone is making the decision not to use that offense as a basis of your actions toward them. In other words, you may not have the ability to wipe it completely from your mind, but you *do* have the ability not to use it against him/her.

Forgiveness is the healing balm for the hurts of a marriage. Learning to apply the ointment of forgiveness will heal the hurts, miraculously. Dare to confess, repent, and seek to lavish forgiveness. This demonstrates the value you place on your relationship with your mate and God.

All too often, we believe that doing things (resolving conflicts, walking in forgiveness, etc.) God's way just won't work, or won't work fast enough. Scripture tells us that if we can only believe, all things are possible (Mark 9:23). Marriage is included in the "all." Although it may seem so at times, your marriage is not the exception to God's Word, and unless you grasp hold of faith for the vision you have for your marriage, you separate yourself from the power source you need to bring it to pass. Only the power of God can change a person, and change is what needs to take place if you are ever going to have the vital, life-giving marriage God so desires for you.

Forgiveness: God's Plan

God has provided a plan for our lives in His word that promises to bless everyone who dares to trust Him and takes Him at his word. Jesus taught His disciples to pray that as they forgave others their trespasses, their heavenly Father would also forgive them. Ephesians 4:31,32 says, *Get rid of all bitterness, rage, anger, harsh words, and slander, as well as all types of malicious behavior. Instead, be kind to each other, tenderhearted, forgiving one another, just as God through Christ has forgiven you* (NLT).

Colossians 3:13 tells us, *You must make allowance for each other's faults and forgive the person who offends you. Remember, the Lord forgave you, so you must forgive others* (NLT).

This is God's plan of forgiveness in action where we acknowledge what He has done for us and pass the kindness on to others in our lives. There is no better place to start and practice God's plan than in our homes with our spouses and offspring.

God lives within us, knows all about us and yet loves and forgives us. Those who live with us in our homes know us best and deserve our best expressions of love and forgiveness. God has set it up such that we cannot say we love him without first loving the people around us.

Avoid Satan's bait of offense. Refuse to allow offenses to take root and cause unforgiveness in your lives, but resist them and recognize them for the tools of Satan that they are. Respond with the love and forgiveness exemplified by God in Christ Jesus. Submit to God and resist the devil. Forgive even as you are forgiven; it is God's will and plan for your life.

There's story of an older lady who had gathered a group of young, newly married women to chat with them about having a happy home. She instructed them in a few areas and then decided to talk about offenses and forgiveness. She stated, "Before my husband and I said, 'I do', I told him that I had a list of things I could never forgive him for. I brought that list with me to share with you, today." They all pulled out their notepads, anxious to write down everything they heard. As she pulled out the list, she carefully unfolded it and showed it to them. It read, "NOTHING!" They were astounded as they were certain they were going to receive some juicy ideas on what they could also use for their lists.

As we sat with one of our pre-marriage coaching couples, we asked them if there were any things the other might do besides physical abuse that would constitute the end of the marriage for them. Adultery was usually the big one, but they listed a few other things. After sorting through that, we encouraged them and admonished them. Our admonition was that as long as we have things for which we have drawn a line in the sand and dared anyone to cross, the devil is going to make sure that those things happen. In other words, we have made ourselves sitting ducks for his target practice. If we could have the attitude of that older lady above and determine that there is nothing the other can do that cannot be forgiven, our enemy will have very little to work with and use against us.

Is there anything for which God will not forgive us? NOTHING! Every bad thing we have ever done or will ever do has been taken care of on the Cross. How dare we try to undo that by withholding forgiveness from each other? Having said that, I understand that forgiveness is not a particularly easy thing for most of us. It requires us putting aside our desire to get even or make someone pay for hurting us. However, because we have the Spirit of God inside us, we have all the power we need to accomplish it. Remember, forgiveness is a choice we make by an act of our will and a desire to obey God's Word. You can do it because you can "do all things through Christ who strengthens" you (Philippians 4:13).

10.
"I'll Take That"

We've all had the experience of being out to dinner with a few people and when the check comes, someone pipes up, "I'll take that," indicating he will take the responsibility of paying the tab. Well, this chapter is about making the choice to be the leader in your home and is especially addressed to the husbands.

The Word of God is very clear in this matter. God has instructed men to be the leaders in their homes. Although we could go into a long explanation of why, it would not change the fact that that is God's will for your family (1 Cor.11:3). Here is another opportunity for you to obey God. Some of you may be rejoicing at this point and thinking, "Great! Now I can really show her who's boss." Indeed, there are many of you who have taken on this leadership role with the misconception that you are to be "king of the castle"; that your wife is now to be at your beck and call 24/7; that you say "Jump," and she says, "How high?"

For those of you who are faint of heart, this may make you cringe a bit: When God commanded men to be the leaders, He intended them to be servants. Ouch! That takes some of the glory out of it, doesn't it? You see, God expects your leadership to be one that is bathed in love. It's not a leadership of domination. The most important part of marital leadership is to love your wife as Christ loved the Church and *gave Himself for it*.

There needs to be a proper balance of responsibility, love, and authority in your marriages.[1] Unselfish love must be maintained at all times. As we have stated before, the things Christ did for the Church were for the benefit of the Church and not for Himself. As you try to emulate the life of Christ and His relationship to the Church in your home, you'll find that your wife will desire for you to take the leadership. It's desirable to have Christ take control of your life when you realize that He wants even more for you than you want for yourself; that He loves you even more than you love yourself. He knows how to bless you in so many more ways than you can think up on your own. You're willing to submit and commit to those you trust and know love you. So again, that balance of responsible authority and unselfish love must be preserved in your marriage.

Let's refer back to Eph. 5:23-24, *For the husband is the head of the wife, as also Christ is the head of the Church…Therefore just as the Church is subject unto to Christ, so let the wives be to their own husbands in everything.* Here the Scripture is clear that God created marriage with only one head; and as the head, the husband is basically the leader of his wife and children.

Admittedly, it's challenging, even difficult for a husband to love his wife as Christ loved the Church because it requires the husband to be fully submitted to Jesus. This is an impossible task without the help of the Holy Spirit. There is nothing in the Word of God that you are capable of doing without the assistance of the Holy Spirit. In order to be submitted, you must develop a relationship with God where you learn to trust Him - even though you don't always know what He is doing in your life; even though you can't see around the corner the way He can, He is always looking out for your good.

In that same way, you should understand why just telling the wife to submit to her husband isn't sufficient. She may do it out of pure obedience to God, but it won't be a true work of the heart until she knows her husband can be trusted with her best interest at heart. And that trust must be developed through relation-building actions that the husband performs day in and day out. True trust is not a gift, neither can it be demanded; it is earned.

Are you wondering what type of actions we mean? The trustworthy husband shows sensitivity to his wife's feelings and concerns.[2] He's keenly aware of her fears. His actions must be void of selfishness, and he must be willing to share his resources and time.

Responsibilities of Leadership

When we talk about leading, we are really describing the process of managing. Managing, as used here, means to handle situations with care and skill while maintaining compliance.[3] The husband has the ultimate responsibility of establishing the direction, organization, and functioning of the family. It's his job to guard the welfare of the family.

Husbands have at least four main responsibilities when it comes to fulfilling their role as leader/manager. We'll list them first then break down each one separately:

- Know your limitations.
- Assess your God-given resources.
- Share the vision.
- Be a doer.

Know your limitations.

As the leader of your home, you must know your limitations. Your greatest understanding of life is to know that without God you can do nothing of eternal value. It is only through the help and guidance of the Holy Spirit that you are able to direct your family in the establishment and execution of the goals, plans, and vision developed by the family.

We have discussed establishing a godly vision for your marriage and then believing God to supply the power to complete the plan. Never forget that the vision is really God- given and without Him, it will not succeed. In John 15:5, Jesus told us, ...*He who abides in me, and I in him, bears much fruit; for without me ye can do nothing.* It is only as you desire to see God's plan accomplished in your lives (and marriage) that you will see victory and glory brought to God in and through your life. David recognized the power of God in his life which resulted in his successful leadership in Psalm 18:35, *You have also given me the shield of Your salvation; Your right hand has held me up, Your gentleness has made me great.*

In knowing your limitations, it's important to develop good judgment. Proverbs 4:5-7 *tells us to: Get wisdom; develop good judgment. Don't forget my words or turn away from them. Don't turn your back on wisdom, for she will protect you. Love her, and she will guard you. Getting wisdom is the wisest thing you can do! And whatever else you do, develop good judgment (NLT).* And then James 3:17 admonishes us, *But the wisdom from above is first of all pure. It is also peace loving, gentle at all times, and willing to yield to others. It is full of mercy and the fruit of good deeds. It shows no favoritism and is always sincere* (NLT).

Many times, in life, including our marriages, we have pursued knowledge and often apprehended it. We have discovered things in books or from various sources and may even recite them to others, but the true understanding of the matter still escapes us. It is one thing to know something and quite another to be able to apply, skillfully, the knowledge possessed at the appropriate time and place.

The Scriptures above encourage us to get wisdom and to value it for its ability to produce positive results in our lives. We have always understood wisdom to be the ability to use the knowledge one has attained in the proper manner. Knowledge, by itself, without awareness of how to use it, can be disastrous, if not useless, in many situations. Knowledge is to be pursued but must be integrated with wisdom to be productive. Therefore, an understanding of God's plan is to get good judgment.

James 1:5: *If you need wisdom, ask our generous God, and he will give it to you. He will not rebuke you for asking* (NLT). The knowledge that blesses us comes from the Word of God and this Scripture tells us that we can obtain wisdom from God for the asking. We must study the Word to gain knowledge, and receive wisdom from God as how to use it. We recognize the wisdom that is from God because the Bible defines it as pure, peace-loving, gentle to, and thoughtful of, others. It is full of mercy, harbors no bias or discrimination, and is full of good deeds and always sincere. As always, God asks us to do nothing without providing the knowledge, wisdom, understanding, and power to be successful.

We can demonstrate good judgment by always acknowledging God in all our endeavors and asking Him just when and where to use the wisdom He has given. Good judgment comes from understanding that without God we can do nothing of value or lasting importance.

We must ask God to direct the actions we take to improve and maintain our relationship with our mates and family. God will educate us as to what is essential, how to execute His Word in wisdom, and allow us to discern the perfect timing and place of implementation.

Assess your God-given resources.

In the process of managing the well-being of the family, the husband is to assess and appreciate the godly resources provided in his wife. God didn't establish the man as a dictator but a leader who uses the wisdom, talents, and strengths of his mate to accomplish the vision God has given. In demonstrating an attitude of unselfish love, he is to accept, analyze, and incorporate the input of his spouse in the decision- making process of the home.

If you understand your limitations and the need for God's help, then you should also recognize God's help in the gift of your mate. God has blessed you with a resource especially designed for your growth and maturity. Proverbs 18:22 says, *He who finds a wife finds a good thing, And obtains favor from the Lord.* Husbands must begin to handle and treat their mates as gifts from God, resulting from their favor with Him. When you begin to thank God for your mate and look for the blessed treasure given in your spouse, your faith in God's faithfulness will release God's power to unite and heal any troubled relationship or esteem issues.

In evaluating your spouse, consider Romans 12:3-5, which says, *...to everyone that is among you, not to think of himself more highly than he ought to think; but to think soberly, as God has dealt to every man the measure of faith. For as we have many members in one body, but all members do not have not the same function: so we, being many, are one body in Christ, and individually members one of another.*

Scripture says that in the process of marriage, two, male and female, become one flesh. Just as the Body of Christ is all one, in your marriage you are one but with different parts making up that one. You have different gifts, talents, abilities, and ultimately responsibilities. With all of this, you need each other to accomplish His plans. As part of the one body, you must learn to respect, appreciate, and honor the gift in the other parts of the body. Your homes should be the first place you come to understand and practice this principle of body-oneness. Ask God to begin to allow you to see your mate through His eyes, to be able to see the valued gift she is and then to allow God's blessing to be effective in your home.

In assessing the gift, that is your wife and the resources she brings to the relationship, it is critical that you take the time to truly know her. It is part of God's vision for you to meet her needs and see to her well-being. It is essential for you to understand your wife, to begin to see how God's purpose for your union will be accomplished. According to Eph. 5:28-29, *So husbands ought to love their own wives as their own bodies; he who loves his wife loves himself. For no one ever hated his own flesh, but nourishes and cherishes it, just as the Lord does the church.*

You must know her needs in order to nourish and cherish her. What are her likes and dislikes? What is she passionate about? What makes her cry? What makes her laugh? What is she excited about? What makes her angry? What is her greatest longing? What is her worst fear?

Encourage your wife to use her God-given capabilities. Use your management skills to put the best person in charge of a given activity. Remember, God's plan is for your marriage to be a union that blesses each of you by completing you, not providing an in-house competitor. Learn to use God's gift wisely.

Ephesians 5:21 addresses the relationship between husbands and wives and gives us directions for success: "*Submit to one another out of reverence for Christ* (NIV)." God is concerned about every aspect of our lives and gives principles, and sometimes-specific instructions, on how to conduct them.

As we look at this verse, we can't help but be impressed with God's desire for us to get along and prosper in our relationship. The directive is for us to yield, submit, honor, and, in some versions, to fit in with each other. He doesn't just leave it at being nice but says that we are to do these things within our marriage bond out of respect for and reverence for Christ. This means that we are conducting our emotional connection with our spouses in a manner of honor, respect, and love, birthed out of obedience and respect for Christ. The NCV version, actually directs us to "Yield to obey each other as you would to Christ". Think about that!

Do you think that God does not know to whom you are married and therefore, couldn't possibly have meant for you to comply in *your* unique situation? God wants couples to respect each other and come to a place where they each are truly the blessing to each other that God intends them to be. God placed you in each other's life to help you serve Him better, not to place a handicap on your potential performance. Trust God to produce a relationship of blessing based on your mutual respect and honor that supersedes your current experience and expectations.

The challenge today, as it will always be, is to dare to obey God's plan and experience the reality of God's appointed best for our lives. God is committed to make His word stand and deliver.

Share the vision.

As the leader of your home, you have developed a vision for your marriage in consultation and collaboration with your wife. You recognize that it is your responsibility to manage the execution of this vision with the help of God and your mate. We now want to encourage you to talk about the vision and share your dreams and thoughts with your spouse.[4]

It is important, as God's chosen leader of your home that you follow the example of Christ who communicated the plan and vision of salvation to His disciples. John 15:15 states, *No longer do I call you servant; for a servant does not know what his master is doing: but I have called you friends; for all things that I have heard from My Father I have made known unto you.* It is the recording of Jesus' teaching and sharing of God's plan that has guided Christians to this day. Jesus communicated both short and long-term goals and objectives that His followers could refer to and be inspired and strengthened by when reviewed.

In the development of your family vision, you have asked God to give you direction. You have modeled your plan after the teaching of Christ and have asked God to bless and empower you to succeed. You now need to share your innermost thoughts and person with your spouse. Your wife is probably already doing this with you, but men are reticent to communicate their inner selves to their wives. Here is where being Christ-like in your home is exemplified. How can you truly work together toward a common goal or vision without sharing your dreams, your fears and expectations, your honest dependence on and respect for each other?

You will find that as you dare to share yourself and your true desires for your family, your spouse will do more of the same. This process of sharing will make you, not only one in flesh but in mind and desires. The more you communicate your thoughts, the more your actions can be properly interpreted and understood. Sharing is one of the day-in and day-out activities that earns the trust of your wife. It will make you and your wife friends and owners of the common goals that will allow you to support one another as never before.

Be a doer.

First Corinthians 11:3 says, *But I would have you know, that the head of every man is Christ; the head of the woman is man; and the head of Christ is God.* God has given you the assignment of being head of your home. Don't abdicate your God-given position, even if encouraged to do so by your wife. We challenge you to accept the responsibility of your assignment with joy, knowing that God and His Word are backing you up.

A good leader leads by example.[5] It requires action on your part. To receive the blessing of following your vision for your family, you must follow the example of Christ in His love, care, and sacrifice. Jesus left His Word as the will and plan of God for your life. James 1:22 instructs, *Be doers of the word, and not hearers only, deceiving yourselves.* Therefore, as you discover and understand the instructions for your life in the Word, you must ask God to help you consistently conform to His will.

It may seem like a daunting task to have to be a living example of Christ's love for the Church, but remember that whoever God calls, He qualifies. You can ask Him, "How are we going to make this happen?" His response is always, "Where you have the will to obey, I will provide the empowerment." Again, you cannot do God's will or Word without faith in His desire and ability to deliver. Trust God to make you the example that your spouse and family need to bring His plan and wonderful blessings to rest and abide in your home.

In acceptance of your responsibility, God has instructed you to love your wife as Christ loved the Church and gave Himself for it. This is an opportunity to be an example of a servant. Christ was willing to, and did, die for us. Husbands sometimes make the declaration they would die for their wives. Interestingly enough, though, those same husbands would have a problem stopping what they were doing to do a chore for their wives. That sounds laughable, but that is how we think sometimes. We'll do the "hard" things, but we're not willing to do the simple ones.

Take a look at Eph. 5:21-22, *Submitting to one another in the fear of God. Wives, submit to your own husbands, as to the Lord.* These Scriptures let us know that submission is a part of all our lives as Christians. God has instructed you to submit to each other as well as wives to their husbands. Note that the submission of the wife is <u>directed by God</u>, not by the husband. It is not the husband's job to demand submission from his wife. Her submission, just as yours, is given in obedience to God. Husbands can be a hindrance to their wives' obedience to God by their failure to be an example of Christ's love in the home. Only as husbands exemplify the love, spirit, and action of Christ will their wives truly begin to see that they (the husbands) are pursuing their wives care.

Husband, trust God to allow you to give of yourself for the needs of your family. Be willing to sacrifice your own needs and desires for it, if necessary. Be willing to set aside consistent time for prayer and the study of God's Word. *You* be the one to lead the family in prayer and devotions. *You* be the one to show honesty and integrity. *You* be the one to demonstrate patience and kindness.

Just because God selected the man to be head doesn't mean God gave him all the brains. As you humbly seek God's direction in prayer, you will find that God has oftentimes already given you help, wisdom, insight, relief, and support in the gifts of your wife. Believe that God had and still has a plan for your marriage that was designed to bless you both.

As you commit to God to be your family's leader, believe Him to lead and direct you by His Spirit and Word. Be willing to accept the responsibility for the good as well as the errant decisions you make. Nothing will influence the fulfillment of your marriage's vision more than your expressed and tireless determination to be an imitator of Christ's love. Be determined to be a doer of God's Word and watch God...*do exceedingly abundantly above all that we ask or think, according to the power that works in us* (Eph. 3:20).

Contentment

1 Timothy 6:6 *[And it is, indeed, a source of immense profit, for] godliness accompanied with contentment (that contentment which is a sense of inward sufficiency) is great and abundant gain (AMPC).*

Today, so many people are under such great pressure to perform and compete that it appears to drain the very joy and God-intended pleasure out of life. There seems to be such a struggle to be first and best at everything we do, but the truth is that not all can or will be first. This is not to say that we don't do our best and pursue excellence in every endeavor but that we realize that doing our best is the goal and desired destination of our passion within God's plan.

The Scripture above makes it clear that godliness with contentment is the source and realization of immense, great, and abundant gain. To put gain in today's terms, it means improvement, advancement, increase, advantage, expansion, addition, achievement, or profit. These are all things that we want to be manifested in our family members and in ourselves. The key word in the Scripture quoted was godliness. Our godliness should be measured by our desire to be identified with and defined as operating within the will of God. The will of God can be found in the Word of God that we are to read, study, and obey. The challenge is for each of us to take the time to develop a personal relationship with God that allows us to know His plan and purpose for us. The struggle is to acknowledge our deviation from God's plan and request His assistance for rectification. You are as unique as your fingerprint, and God has a use and destiny for you that are equally unique. We must come to a position of clarity regarding who we believe God desires us to be.

It is only as we fulfill our God-given purpose that doing our best really matters. Being in our place, doing the tasks God designed and prepared just for us is true contentment. When we know our place based on God's personalized design and will for us, then we can have the sense of inward sufficiency available only through God's insight. When we do our best and practice a spirit of excellence in performing our assigned life task, we can believe God for great gain and contentment.

True contentment is obtainable only through bringing pleasure to the heart of God by doing what we were designed to do with faith-filled commitment. Then no matter what life brings, we can say with the Apostle Paul, "Not that I speak in regard to need, for I have learned in whatever state I am, to be content", (Philippians 4:11). Contentment is being in the center of God's will doing the best you can with His help.

11.
The J-J-Joy of S-S-Submission

Well, ladies, here we go. We told you that marriage was not for the faint of heart, and now here we are talking about submission. It's hard to say the word sometimes without stuttering, isn't it and then to call it a joy?! It's probably one of the most controversial and misunderstood concepts of a Christian marriage. It's understandable why the secular world can't handle it; but when you can get clear comprehension and insight from the Word of God, there's no good reason to reject it. Most of what you've heard on this subject is opinion, not truth. But we're going to point you directly to the Word of God.

When husband and wife are conflicted about their roles in the relationship, the results are chaos, confusion, and strife. We want to clear up the bewilderment and make this subject more palatable because, believe it or not, God knew what He was doing when He set this mandate in order.

The very word "submission" strikes fear and disdain in the hearts of most intelligent, independent-thinking women. It conjures up words like: domination, subservience, inferiority, doormat, insignificance, and the list could go on and on.[1] Certainly, this whole area has been sorely abused and perverted. Nevertheless, God intended it to be a blessing.

Now, here are some new words to ponder: stress-free living, peace of mind, freedom, rest. Women are so stressed in this day and age, they think the only way to experience those things is to go on a vacation, *"by myself."* As incredible as it sounds, God intended submission to be a permanent vacation from the daily stresses of life. If embraced properly, it can be one of the most carefree ways of life possible.

In the previous chapter, we discussed the importance of the husband taking his role as head of household seriously while taking on the character of Christ to do so. Now, we will delve into how wives can take their proper place in the relationship and stand alongside their husbands with an attitude of submission.

Let's do an Ephesians reminder, *Wives, submit to your own husbands, as to the Lord. For the husband is head of the wife, as also Christ is head of the church; and He is the Savior of the body. Therefore, just as the church is subject to Christ, so let the wives be to their own husbands in everything.* (Eph. 5:22-24). We also need to take a look at Colossians 3:18: *Wives, be subject to your husband – subordinate and adapt yourselves to them – as is right and fitting and your proper duty in the Lord* (AMPC).

As much as we would like to sometimes, we cannot reconstruct the above verses to read: *Wives submit yourselves to your husbands when they are acting like the*

Lord. It's your responsibility to do so even when they are acting like jerks.

You must come to an understanding that submission to authority is a normal part of everyday life. Everyone has someone to whom they must submit in order for things to get done: employees to bosses; military personnel to commanding officers; citizens to the law. Even our President must be accountable to the other branches of the government or risk impeachment. For some reason, though, the idea of submitting to someone we know intimately or consider our equal makes us bristle.

When someone decides to rebel and not submit to the powers that be, there are consequences. It may cost their job, their freedom, or very life. We'll discuss more about this notion of rebellion later. But first, let's define submission.

To submit is to humbly and voluntarily yield and intelligently obey an ordained power or authority.[2] It is an attitude of the heart, an attitude of yieldedness.[3] It is choosing to go along with someone else's decision even when you don't agree with it. Ninety percent of the time, it will go against your flesh especially when it comes to submitting to your husband. This is probably because, generally speaking, women think that they are smarter than men. However, God did not create this plan based on intelligence. God created man first and gave him dominion or authority over all other creation, including woman. He could just as easily have switched it around at the time when Eve convinced Adam to disobey God in the garden and eat the forbidden fruit. Instead, He reminded Eve that her husband would be her leader even though she would want to control him. *And you will desire to control your husband, but he will rule over you. (Gen. 3:16, NLT).* THAT, ladies and gentlemen, was part of the curse. Women have been fighting that issue ever since then. But thanks be to God who has redeemed us from the curse because of Jesus. Now you don't have to live in that state anymore. You have a choice. If you have the desire to do it God's way, He will empower you.

Jesus was our ultimate example of submission. He was thoroughly submitted to the Father, so much so that it cost His life. He anguished in the garden; and even sought the Father three times as to whether there could be another way to redeem mankind (Matt. 26:39-44). Obviously, this was going to be the most painful experience Jesus was ever going to endure, but He was willing to do it because He was submitted to His Father's will. Father God had the final word. Imagine what would have happened if Jesus had rebelled. God forbid!!

Husbands have the final word. Here's A situation: You have to make a decision regarding something important. You and your husband discuss it and discuss it, but you just can't seem to come to a resolution. You obviously disagree how it should be handled. You think his suggestion is unworthy but your idea is brilliant. Your husband finally decides it should go a certain way. You don't agree, but you comply. That is submission.

Submission: A Place of Honor and Protection

Submission costs you something, but the benefits are far greater. God never intended for women to experience the kind of stress that goes along with living in this society. Therefore, He established the idea of male (husband) headship for your protection and the harmony of your homes. God is not against women. He is not holding a grudge against them for what happened in the garden. He holds women in high esteem. In fact, He calls the Church the "Bride of Christ." However, He knows that women are vulnerable physically, emotionally, and spiritually, just as the Bride of Christ is at large. When the Church is submitted to Jesus, we live in peace, our needs are met, and we are able to rest in Him. On the other hand, when we think we can do things our own way or think we have a better way, we find ourselves frustrated and miserable. It's the same when it comes to obeying your husband. Submitting yourself to his authority gives you a great deal of protection from the ravages of stress. The truth is, unlike the lyrics to the song, "I am Woman," women are not invincible.

If, of course, you'd rather take care of yourself, God will let you, but you will suffer for it. "God intended for a husband to stand between his wife and the world, absorbing many of the physical, emotional, and spiritual attacks that would come against her.[4] If he abandons or abdicates that role or if you steal it from him, your home suffers great loss.

Never forget that our example is Jesus, Himself. Think about the glory He left to come to earth for our salvation. He chose to do this in obedience to His Father because it was for our good. He didn't have the mindset that He was degrading Himself.

The wife is to submit to her husband the same way she submits to Christ. It is critical that you understand that, ultimately, when you submit to your husband, you are submitting to God. When you send your children to school, they are now under the authority of that classroom teacher, and you expect them to be obedient to him/her. If, however they decide not to obey, who are they actually disobeying? Yes, their parents! God is the One to whom you must answer for your disobedience. He doesn't expect you to submit because your husband is perfect and has perfect wisdom. Rather, God expects you to trust that if He placed him as your leader, God would equip your husband as he seeks *God's* wisdom. This is why praying for your husband is essential.

One important thing to remember is that God never asked women to obey their husbands at the risk of committing sin. In other words, when your husband's request is in blatant disobedience to God's written Word, God expects you to obey His Word, first. The Scripture clearly states that the wife's obedience is "in the Lord," – not blind obedience, but God-centered obedience.

It's Your Choice

There are only two responses to God's edict to submit, and you get to choose: Obedience or rebellion. Obviously, when you choose to obey God, you reap the benefits of peace, satisfaction, tranquility, and joy. However, when you decide you are not going to obey the Word because you think you have a better idea, you are in rebellion against God, not just your husband. I Samuel 15:22-23 tells us, *But Samuel replied, What is more pleasing to the Lord: your burnt offerings and sacrifices or your obedience to His voice? Obedience is far better than sacrifice. Listening to Him is much better than offering the fat of rams. Rebellion is as bad as the sin of witchcraft, and stubbornness is as bad as worshiping idols* (NLV). Whoa! That's pretty strong.

Some of you are probably saying at this point, "I would submit if my husband would fulfill his part." His part, of course, is to love his wife as Christ loves the Church. We covered, in depth, what that entails in the previous chapter. However, remember we also mentioned that each of you is expected to give your one hundred percent whether or not your mate is doing his. The husband is commanded to extend Christ-like love toward his wife even if she NEVER submits. The wife is commanded to submit even if her husband doesn't demonstrate Christ-like love.

Wives of unresponsive Christian husbands and wives of unsaved husbands need to refer to the same Scripture in I Peter 3:1, *Wives, likewise, be submissive to your own husbands, that even if some do not obey in word, they, without a word, may be won by the conduct of their wives.* This leaves no room for, "I will if he will."

What about women with very strong personalities? Indeed, there are some of you out there who just naturally have a "take charge" kind of attitude and feel more comfortable taking matters into your own hands. It's who you are, and it's difficult to just lay that aside. Well, the truth is that you don't have to lay it completely aside, but you will have to temper it by an act of your will. Understand that because of the strength of your personality, you have the capability to emasculate your husband. Submission should not diminish your personality but enhance it. The husband who is a good manager (which is what being the head of household really boils down to) will recognize the gifts God has placed in you and appreciate your insights. You must learn to express your opinion and desires in a non-threatening manner which will require some finesse on your part. If you allow him to take his rightful place, he will probably, in many cases, see things from your perspective.

Since husbands are mere men and not perfect, they always run the risk of making unwise decisions. Is there any recourse? Absolutely! PRAY! Prayer is so much more powerful than nagging. It's so much more effective than berating. You have the power of this universe (and every other universe) at your disposal through prayer. Prayer can change your husband's heart much better than you can in your own strength.

When it's all said and done, this one thing is sure: Accepting the role of submission to your husband's authority requires spiritual maturity. When you line yourself up with God's Word, you will begin to see Him move in miraculous ways. We can't always say that God's plans are crystal clear to us and that we understand everything He is doing. We can say, however, with great assurance, that God is always looking out for our good. If you are not yet convinced, let Jeremiah 29:11 be a personal word for you, *For I know the thoughts and plans that I have for you, says the Lord, thoughts and plans for welfare and peace, and not for evil, to give you hope in your final outcome* (AMPC).

When you stop fighting God's plan and work in concert with it, you can expect Him to be there for you at every turn and in every instance.

The Battle of the Sexes

Genesis 1:27 *(NLT) So God created human beings in his own image. In the image of God he created them;* **male and female** *he created them.*

Did you know that the first battle of the sexes began in the Garden of Eden?

Eve convinced Adam to partake of the fruit in the garden they were not supposed to touch. Why do you think the serpent saw Eve as an easy mark? Here's a theory: Women have a tendency to make decisions, many times, from an emotional standpoint first. Logic typically follows later. Of course, this is a generalization, so you may be the exception. Satan was able to appeal to her emotional side by pointing out how nice the fruit looked and helping her to imagine how good it will taste and how it will make her feel. Because men tend to see things more logically first (again, a generalization), Satan would have had a harder time tempting Adam. I think he (Adam) would have reminded Satan of what God specifically said to him and more easily resisted.

Satan was very deliberate in choosing Eve to put his plan into motion because he knew that if he could persuade her to eat the fruit, she would be more influential to Adam. It was at that point that it was established how powerful a woman's influence was.

Eve won the battle of the sexes but ultimately lost. Her decision caused Adam to sin and thus caused mankind to lose close fellowship with God. The result of that costly sin was a curse that God placed on their lives: "Then he said to the woman, 'I will sharpen the pain of your pregnancy, and in pain you will give birth. And you will desire to control your husband, but he will rule over you.' And to the man he said, 'Since you listened to your wife and ate from the tree whose fruit I commanded you not to eat, the ground is cursed because of you. All your life you will struggle to scratch a living from it (Gen. 3:16-17, NLT)'" At this point, God banishes them from the Garden.

Perhaps, this gives us some understanding of why men and women are always in a battle to see who will take the lead in a relationship. It's because of the curse. But remember, if you are born again, you are no longer under the curse. We have been redeemed from it (Gal. 3:13), so we have the grace and ability to receive strength to resist the temptation to battle over dominion. As husband and wife, we can live in harmony with each other and experience the blessings of obedience to God's Word instead of the curse of disobedience.

God's best is that we live a life of peace, free from strife, walking in Jesus' promise of abundant life.

12.
Let's Talk

Probably every book on marriage you pick up will have at least one chapter on communication. Well, our book will be no exception. Until people get it right, we'll always have to talk about it because it's an area where men and women have some of their greatest battles. Men and women have different needs when it comes to communicating. Understanding those differences can be extremely helpful and perhaps cut down on some of the battle scars.

One of the best books we have recently read on this topic is, *Men Are Clams. Women Are Crowbars* by Dr. David Clarke. His basic premise is that men have a difficult time with communication, and women do everything in their power to try to amend that by forcing the issue.[1] These methods, of course, do not work very well, and consequently, conflicts erupt. We highly recommend this book if you would like a further study on this particular aspect of communications.

In this chapter, we'll concentrate on the importance of just plain talking to each other. God never intended for us, as humans, to live in solitude. He created us to have fellowship with Him and each other. The greatest opportunity for fellowship, once we're married, is with our spouse; or at least it should be.

One of the great hindrances to good husband-wife communication is that men and women have been socialized to mistrust each other. Many times, you feel that your mate cannot be trusted with knowledge about you. The thought is: they may someday use it against you. This is so unfortunate since the marriage relationship was designed to be the most intimate one on the planet. Intimacy involves much more than mere sex.

We covered a great deal about spending time with each other and how that translates into good communication in our chapter on "Being Best Friends," but there is still more to be said.

Good communication must start with the things you say to each other on a daily basis. In order to create an atmosphere of sharing and intimacy, you must be mindful of your words to each other. You can't afford to be careless. Remember, your home is not a "God-free zone." God is interested in every aspect of your life and wants to be invited in. Proverbs 18:21 tells us, *Death and life are in the power of the tongue....* Your words must be habitually life-filled. Some expression of love should be used each day. This can be done any number of ways: notes in the lunches, love letters left on the pillow. We know of one couple who were actually in competition (This is the good kind.) with each other to see who could come up with the most creative way to say "I love you." Some of their ideas were outrageous, but they had fun doing it. And you'd better believe it strengthened their relationship.

Become the president of each other's fan club. In other words, root for each other. Lavish each other with words of encouragement and adoration. Besides declaring your love, try to say at least one encouraging thing each day. It's easy to think of discouraging things to say. We get discouraging messages all day, every day from others. Let your home be the one place where you know someone is going to lift you up. Words like, "I'm proud of you" and "You're doing a good job," go a long way in the day and age in which we live. When you know that the people in your home have your back, it makes it so much easier to open up and share who you are with them.

Listening is one of the most important aspects of communication. And it's not the kind of listening you might think. The best listening you can do is paying attention to the little things your spouse says to you throughout the day. You may be having a nonchalant conversation at the breakfast table, when your wife says, "I'm a little tired today. Well, let me hurry up and clean up these breakfast dishes." Because you're paying attention, and you're listening, you say, "Oh, don't worry about those. I'll take care of it. You relax for a minute." Without saying another word, you have just communicated to your wife that you *do* pay attention to her needs, and you care even about the little things. Or your husband mentions that he has a long list of things he needs to get done today, and he happens to glance out the window to the garage and says (almost as a whisper), "Man, I need to get that dirty car washed." Even though what he said was almost inaudible, you recognized that is one thing *you* can take care of and lessen his load. When you do it without even telling him you're going to, he recognizes that you were listening; he begins to feel that you truly do desire to be his helper and partner. This is setting the tone in your home that produces an environment of trust. When you trust, you share. When you share, you're communicating. How glorious!

In order for you to achieve success in your marriage relationship, you must walk in agreement with your mate. Amos 3:3, reads: *Can two walk together unless they are agreed?* Agreement is "harmony of opinion, action or character; an arrangement as to a course of action."[2] In order to reach common goals and objectives, agreement must take place. Notice from our definitions that this is not done by osmosis. It requires talking. It requires communication which is crucial in the development of the vision for your marriage.

When Conflicts Come...

A natural outgrowth, in the process of attempting to come to agreement as how to develop and execute the vision God has given you, is conflict. This is not the time to become discouraged. If you can remember that this is a natural thing that occurs in all relationships – marriage or otherwise – you will be prepared to deal effectively.

If necessary, refer back to the chapter on "The Two

Marriage Killers." When you throw pride and selfishness out, you'll remember to attack the issue and not your mate. Your purpose will be to solve the problem and not to destroy or belittle your spouse.

When offenses come (and they will), it's important to know how to resolve them. If you recognize that things are not quite right, be willing to initiate dialog. If you are the offender, be honest enough to admit it to your mate, and make the correction. Even if you are the one who has been offended, be willing to take the first step toward resolution. Stewing and pouting are nonproductive and can be damaging.

It's extremely important to find the right time to discuss issues. So be sure not to waste your words by trying to deal with something when no one is really listening. An inappropriate time would be, for instance, while your mate is engrossed in particular television program or other activity. Unless it's an emergency, it's not really fair to make him/her have to choose between you and that activity. Other unsuitable times are during illness or just before leaving for work.

When you start the process, be as nonthreatening as possible. Proverbs 15:1 says, *A gentle answer turns away wrath, but harsh words stir up anger* (NLT). Attitude and tone of voice make a huge difference. Words like: "There are a few things you need to know!" or "There are a few issues we need to get settled!" are phrases that, said the wrong way, prepare the other person to become defensive because they will feel under attack.

Remember to only discuss the issue at hand. Don't

dig up the past; don't use this as a time to assassinate your spouse's character.

Determine to hear what is actually being said and not what you think is being said. Proverbs 18:35 puts it this way, *What a shame, what folly, to give advice before listening to the facts* (NLT)! In other words, keep listening until you hear all the facts. This will prevent you from forming a response too soon.

Some of the best counsel on communication during conflict can be found in Eph. 4:25-27, 29-32: *So stop telling lies. Let us tell our neighbors the truth, for we are all parts of the same body. And "don't sin by letting anger control you" Don't let the sun go down while you are still angry, for anger gives a foothold to the devil. ... Don't use foul or abusive language. Let everything you say be good and helpful, so that your words will be an encouragement to those who hear them. And do not bring sorrow to God's Holy Spirit by the way you live. Remember, he has identified you as his own, guaranteeing that you will be saved on the day of redemption. Get rid of all bitterness, rage, anger, harsh words, and slander, as well as all types of evil behavior. Instead, be kind to each other, tenderhearted, forgiving one another, just as God through Christ has forgiven you.* (NLT).

How could anything be clearer? God has prescribed a way for you to deal with your loved one during times of discord. There is never any reason for the settling of disagreements to become shouting matches or mean spirited.

The bottom line is this: Most of the things we

quibble over are totally unnecessary; most times they can be ignored. When you do have serious issues, deal with them using great care not to damage the love relationship. The goal is to remain one in purpose; that your hearts stay open to one another. Remember, your spouse is your beloved, not your enemy.

13.
What God Wants You to Know About Sex

The first thing we need to do is go straight to the Word of God on the matter of sex. Hebrews 13:4 says, *Marriage is honorable in all, and the bed undefiled; but whoremongers and adulterers God will judge* (KJV).

This chapter gives a brief overview on the issue of sex in marriage. If you'd like a more in-depth study on this subject, see the Suggested Reading list at the end of this book.

What God wants you to know about sex is that it is, as marriage, His creation. In the Scripture above, the word "bed" derives from a Greek word that means cohabitation; by implication, the male sperm.[1] In other words we are talking about sexual intimacy. God's view of marriage and sex between husband and wife is that it is to be held in honor, esteemed worthy, precious, something of great price, and especially dear. We live in an age where sex is considered just another recreational activity that anybody can participate in. The world has taken sex out of it place of honor and sacredness and placed it on the garbage heap.

God created sex for married couples only, and He

intended it for enjoyment as well as for the production of godly offspring. It is part of His plan to bless us. It's an ordained gift to enhance intimacy and the physical process of oneness. It's meant to be both holy and intensely enjoyable.[2] Look at Proverbs 5:18-19: *May your fountain be blessed, and may you rejoice in the wife of your youth. A loving doe, a graceful deer— may her breasts satisfy you always, may you ever be intoxicated with her love* (NIV).

Sexual fulfillment in marriage is another one of those areas where God needs to be placed front and center. Remember the "God-free zone"? It doesn't exist here, either. If problems arise in this area, you want the Creator's guidance and help to sort them out. After all, He knows more about it than you do. We have been bombarded with so many negative images of sex from the media to people we may know, personally. This has resulted in having a lot of shame associated with sex. That was never God's plan. That has, perhaps, made it difficult to go to God for His assistance in this area. However, God wants us to feel free to invite Him to help us experience satisfaction and gratification.

God, in His wisdom, created needs and desires in us that can only be satisfied in the sexual union. We must recognize these needs and do all we can to fulfill them for each other. When a husband and wife take hold of the concept of meeting the other's needs and begin to do everything they can to do that, they are sure to develop an exciting relationship.

Some have asked the question, "What is considered

a normal sex life?" We would never tell anyone how frequently they should be united intimately or what *normal* is, but we will give you Scripture and verse. In I Corinthians 7:3-5, it reads: *The husband should not deprive his wife of sexual intimacy, which is her right as a married woman, nor should the wife deprive her husband. The wife gives authority over her body to her husband, and the husband also gives authority over his body to his wife. So do not deprive each other of sexual relations. The only exception to this rule would be the agreement of both husband and wife to refrain from sexual intimacy for a limited time, so they can give themselves more completely to prayer...*(NLT).

Now, there are two principles at work in the above verses. First, you give up the control of your body to your spouse in the area of sex. Is this saying that you are to force each other to have sex? Certainly not! It simply means that when you withhold sex from each other, you are in disobedience to God's Word. It should be understood, however, that all sexual activity must be consensual and free of guilt, shame, and condemnation. It is important, also, that you understand that when you do decide to take time away from each other sexually for spiritual consecration, again, it must be agreeable to both of you. The period of time should be agreed upon as well. In other words, don't make an announcement; get permission.

The next thing you see in these Scriptures is that, although it doesn't say how often, it is obvious that it is something you're not to take long periods of time away from.

Although sex is not the most important part of your marriage, it is a critical component. Allow God to be the Lord of your bedroom. Don't try to hide from Him there. Don't close any doors to Him, and watch Him move on your behalf.

14.

Take Heart, Be Encouraged

Our desire, in developing this book, was to encourage people to believe God for successful marriages. In all actuality, we could easily sum up the how-to of a successful marriage in three words: **Do God's Word!!** It's really just that simple. Most people seem, however, to prefer some clever method or technique with steps one, two and three. Well, here are your three steps:

- Study God's Word.
- Believe God's Word
- Apply (or live) God's Word

It's really no more mysterious than that.

What we have tried to present is a framework from which you can launch your own search in the Word of God for instructions on marriage. View your union as a miniature version of God's relationship to you. Try to emulate the love you received from your Heavenly Father with your actions toward your spouse and family. What greater gift can you give your loved ones than to demonstrate what God has done for you through Jesus.

We come into this world with all kinds of character flaws, idiosyncrasies, quirks, and most of all sin. When we accept the Lord Jesus, God chooses to forgive us and receive you as clean. We still have the quirks, and we still sin, but God continues to readily forgive when we ask Him to. His love is not put on hold until we get it right. He continues to be everything we need to help us get it right. We are to do that for our mate.

As you make the commitment to "do the Word," the Bible will become one enormous marriage manual that will address every area of your life. The good news is that it will never become obsolete. It doesn't matter whether we are in the old or new millennium, God's Word doesn't change. Jesus told us that He is the same yesterday, today and forever (Hebrews 13:8).

If God wants you to have a vital and exciting marriage, you can have it through faith. All you need to know is God's will and be willing to receive and obey. Look, listen, and dig for biblical principles that will strengthen your relationship in every area, then, pray for insight on how to bless your mate and marriage as a whole. If you are married, the greatest human love object you should have is your spouse. Learn to practice and perfect your love-walk with him/her, then, spread it abroad.

Jesus instructed us in Luke 18:1 that, *men always ought to pray....* All we want you to learn is that God is ready and willing to answer and address your prayers concerning bringing His plan and purpose for your marriage into manifestation in your life.

Marriage is not for the faint of heart because it takes courage and tenacity to do the hard things to get to the great things. Marriage is, indeed, a great thing. Be willing to do the hard things, and you will see God do what He promised. We guarantee, you will find yourself praising Him for His mighty deeds.

The Heart of the Matter

As you have read this book, you have noticed that we have used a lot of Scripture. Marriage, the way God designed it, is a spiritual journey; and the only way to have success in it is to do it God's way. It's impossible to truly do it His way without His Spirit.

If you are reading this book and know that you do not have a personal relationship with God through His Son, Jesus, you can make that happen right now. It's not difficult, but it will change your life forever. All you need to do is confess with your mouth that Jesus is Lord and believe in your heart that God raised Him from the dead, and you will be saved (Romans 10:9-10). If you desire to have the Spirit of God dwelling on the inside of you to help you to accomplish His will, simply pray this prayer aloud:

> "God, I thank you that you love me. I believe that Jesus is your only Son and that He is Lord. I believe He died for my sins and that you raised Him from the dead. Please forgive me for the sins I have committed and accept me as your child. Thank you for making me clean and saving me. I belong to you from now on. In Jesus' name, I pray. Amen."

Encouraging Marriage Thoughts
(90-day Devotional)

We have compiled ninety devotionals relating to marriage and interpersonal relationships. It is our desire to provide you with inspirational thoughts that may provoke you to examine yourself and your relationships for improvement and growth opportunities.

There are only ninety devotionals because we wanted to have enough for you to form a habit of reading and embracing a marriage challenge with your spouse and yet not be overwhelming. How would we suggest you use this devotional?

- Make a commitment to read a thought each day for ninety days with your spouse. It will take no more than fifteen minutes. Choose a time agreeable to both of you.

- After you have read the devotional, pray asking God to help you see and understand how you may change personally to make your relationship improve. Ask God to open your heart and mind to hear and obey whatever He is directing you to do.

- Commit to ask and believe God to assist you in applying the principles you believe are speaking to you regarding your relationships.

- Believe that God wants to and will walk along with you

through the growth process of enhancing your life and marriage.

- Remember to do your part and trust God to do His in you and your mate.

DAY ONE
There is No Perfect Marriage!
(Pam)

Ephesians 4:32 *(NLT)* ...*be kind to each other, tenderhearted, forgiving one another, just as God through Christ has forgiven you.*

Ephesians 5:1-2 *(NLT) Imitate God, therefore, in everything you do, because you are his dear children. Live a life filled with love, following the example of Christ. He loved us and offered himself as a sacrifice for us, a pleasing aroma to God.*

Does that statement discourage or challenge you? I hope it challenges you because, although there is no perfect marriage, every marriage can be amazing with the proper care.

How many couples have we all known that seemed perfect for each other only to find out later that they had divorced? What appeared to be perfect eventually turned sour or even tasteless. Why does this happen? Why do some marriages succeed while others fail? The simplest answer is that somewhere along the line, someone decided to stop obeying God's Word.

I was one of those people who used to think that in order for a marriage to be successful, it had to be perfect. I now realize that success is not perfection. The correct spelling of success in marriage is W-O-R-K.

And it's hard work at that! I very soon discovered that the "perfection" I was looking for didn't happen automatically just because we were so much in love.

One of the reasons that we cannot find perfection in marriage is because each of us is on a continual growth path, and we discover new things about ourselves each day. This is the reason we cannot afford to sleepwalk through our relationship. If we do, we'll miss some very important clues in determining how to work with and get along with our spouse. The following poem by an anonymous author says it very well:

No Marriage is Perfect

Marriage is a daily creation, not a packaged product.
Marriage is like a child who needs to be picked up and hugged and given personal attention,
Marriage is not something simple to be weighed against expectations and rejected when found short.
Marriage needs a delicate touch and patient treatment.
The handling of it cannot always be thought out ahead of time.
Often the way must be felt slowly, gently, in the dark.
The danger is not in the dark.
The danger is in losing hope or patience.

If you are struggling in your marriage relationship, check to see if you have forgotten to give it personal attention. Are you holding on to hurts? Are the expectations you have of your mate (or even yourself) unrealistic. Have you laid aside the Word of God and done things in your own strength? If you answered yes to any of these questions, please understand that it's not too late to make a course correction and get back on track. No one wants a failed marriage; unfortunately, not everyone is willing to do what it takes to triumph beyond the struggle. I challenge you to be the one who will do the hard work and, indeed, discover the joy of a successful, amazing marriage albeit not a perfect one.

DAY TWO
Partners Not Competitors
(Adrian)

Genesis 2:24 *Therefore a man shall leave his father and mother and be joined to his wife, and they shall become one flesh.*

Here is when God first presented Eve to Adam in the Garden of Eden. This Scripture is an excellent directive for couples today and will allow our marriages to be the blessing that God always intended for them to be and still does. The idea was for the husband and wife to leave the ties of their parental family as the primary focus of life's direction and redirect their focus on a new family unit formed with their marriage partners.

Today, it seems that many marriages have given everyone and everything else priority over their mates in determining life's direction and goals. Some have even allowed outside influences, other than God, to define their definition of success and purpose in life. The end result of this shifting of priorities and purpose has caused many couples to become competitors instead of partners in achieving their God-given goals and purpose. God created the institution of marriage to bless both husband and wife with a partner who would facilitate their serving God better together than apart.

This requires us to believe that God had and still has

a divine purpose for our marriages. That divine purpose was to allow both partners to achieve His call upon their lives and be a support, not a hindrance, to each other. This requires that we seek God for His purpose for bringing us together and realize that He knows the individual call assigned to each of us. When we learn to appreciate and respect the God-given call and talents invested by God in each of us, we will be less inclined to selfishly ignore the gift given to us in our mate. Only when we do not honor God in each other, can we smother the gift and purpose designed by God for the one flesh created in the marriage union. By becoming our mate's competitor, we miss God's blessing.

Let the one flesh of your marriage union represent the understanding of the God-given plan for your union. Let me describe it as the "US Factor"; that is, to pursue the purpose and divine goal of God for you as a couple.

DAY THREE
Transparency
(Adrian)

Galatians 6:2 *(AMP) Carry one another's burdens and in this way you will fulfill the requirements of the law of Christ [that is, the law of Christian love].*

I remember when I first met my wife and the joy of finding a friend who brought such happiness to my life. We were committed to each other and desired to help the other achieve what we believed was God's call upon our lives. It was and is our belief that God allowed us to be joined in marriage to help us please Him better together than we could ever realize by being apart.

Our relationship began with trying to learn and appreciate as much about each other as possible. It was so much fun and fascinating to discover the likes and dislikes, visions and plans for the future that we had made as individuals. Then to lovingly handle each other's desires, always wanting to preserve them where possible and combine them to allow each of us to feel and experience the value, respect, and honor of an open and transparent relationship. We realized what it meant to assist the other in pursuing our determination to please God and each other.

We had come to an awareness that God had placed

us in each other's lives to be His physical and emotional representative of love. God knows everything about us better than we know ourselves; yet in marriage, we must learn the intimate details of our mates over time. This is where transparency is so vital to the health and continued growth and maturity of our marriages. Being open with one another allows us to not only stumble upon but to see the weaknesses and strengths of the other. Openness reveals the dreams and nightmares of your mate for nurturing, protection, and sharing. Closeness is very difficult, if not impossible, without the vulnerability of open and honest communications - honest talk that is spoken always in love with a desire to bring healing.

God helps because he knows everything, but He still asks us to ask for help. In order for us, or our partners, to help one another, we must share everything. Remember, we want to know so that we can demonstrate the love of God toward our spouse. This requires a selfless attitude that invites the presence and help of God into our lives. We must stay on task as God's representatives and assistants to help our mates achieve their destinies and God-given purposes. You will only be able to do this if you believe God is working for your good through your mate. This requires you to be wholly committed to love your mate, as you believe God loves you. You are one in Christ.

To accomplish this, you must encourage each other and spend time weekly sharing goals, aspirations, and dreams, as well as hurts, failures, and feelings of inadequacy, mistakes, sins, and victories. Be vulnerable enough to communicate what may seem obvious: that you love each other and are committed to the other's success in life.

DAY FOUR
Imprisoned by a Grudge
(Pam)

Proverbs 17:9 *(NLT) Love prospers when a fault is forgiven, but dwelling on it separates close friends*

Why is it so difficult to let go of the hurts inflicted upon us? Being hurt by the people we love, most especially our mates, can be hard to overcome. But why is that? Could it be just a matter of acting out our natural impulse to protect ourselves, or is it a need for retaliation? Is it a matter of withholding forgiveness to use as a power tool?

There is a part of our natural humanness that wants to protect itself from future hurts and pains. Think of falling off a horse. It is painful and disturbing. The memory of such an incident may cause you to never want to get on another horse as long as you live. However, what is typically said? "You have to get back on the horse, immediately." Why is that? If you don't, you will have the opportunity for the memory to linger; and as you dwell on it, the fear of it grows more intense. The same thing is true in our relationships. When we are hurt, unless we freely forgive quickly, we have a tendency to dwell on it giving the devil a foothold and causing a rift. Not only that, but the pain of the offense intensifies the longer we hold onto it.

Focusing on an offense imprisons us. It invades our thought life; and if we are not careful, we will start planning our retaliation. It allows the enemy (Satan) to convince us that we have power over the offender by not forgiving. The fact is, we couldn't be more wrong. Sometimes, it's difficult to understand, but the inability to forgive does not affect the offender as much as it affects us. We are the ones who suffer. It tears us up on the inside. Consider the following quote: "The failure to forgive fosters *debilitating attitudes of resentment and rage*. Many research studies show significant correlation between resentment and anger and the reduction of the efficiency of the immune system--the effect of which is to increase our vulnerability to illnesses ranging from the common cold to AIDS. Other people, unforgiven, literally make us sick" (Robert Caldwell, *The Difficult and Compelling Art of Forgiving*)[1]

Because we have been born again, we no longer have to rely on our "natural humanness" to muster up the courage to let go of a grudge we may be holding against our beloved. Remember that, "you belong to God, my dear children…" (1 John 4:4, NLT), so we have the power of God upon which to rely.

Let's break free from the prison of grudge holding. Let's always be willing to give to our mates the same thing God gives to us – unlimited forgiveness. Let's allow our love to prosper by forgiving our spouses faults. Besides, we probably have many more than they do.

DAY FIVE
Ending the Tug of War
(Pam)

Tug of war is a sport that directly pits two teams against each other in a test of strength. Another definition is a struggle for supremacy. Now imagine it as metaphor for a husband and wife who constantly pull against or compete with each other to get his or her own way in a marriage. Think it works? Of course not!

It's so unfortunate, but that is how a huge number of marriages can be described: a tug of war. Sometimes the husband is stronger in his stance, and he gets what he wants. Other times, the wife is the one who pulls with the most force and "wins".

There is nothing wrong with a little fun competition in games, but when that carries over into your everyday encounters, trouble is not too far behind. When a couple joins together in the covenant of marriage, and they don't have similar goals, or they entered into the relationship for selfish reasons, they pick up the rope called life and begin to pull against each other. When this happens, you have no power in which to fight against the enemy of your marriage, Satan.

How about changing your strategy? Get on the same team! How about joining your forces against Satan's threats and tactics? Now imagine yourselves together on one end of the rope and the devil on the other. You may think that he is too strong for just the two of you; but don't forget – you have a secret weapon at your disposal. It's called agreement. The Bible says, "I also tell you this: If two of you agree here on earth concerning anything you ask, my Father in heaven will do it for you (Matthew 18:19 NLT)." Even more importantly, the Power of God is available to assist you and give you the advantage.

Remember, God put you together to be stronger together. Lay aside your selfish needs and desires and concentrate on building an unstoppable team whose desire is to please God and each other.

DAY SIX
Cooperation
(Adrian)

Ecclesiastes 4:9-12 *Two are better than one, Because they have a good reward for their labor. For if they fall, one will lift up his companion. But woe to him who is alone when he falls, For he has no one to help him up. Again, if two lie down together, they will keep warm; But how can one be warm alone? Though one may be overpowered by another, two can withstand him. And a threefold cord is not quickly broken.*

This Scripture is applicable to any covenant friendship but especially pertinent to a husband and wife team. The dictionary simply defines cooperation as working together and secondly as compliance. As we look around our world today, the old cliché that said, "something is easier said than done" comes to mind. Maybe you have experienced the difficulty of simply trying to work together with your spouse. The synonyms listed with the definition were assistance, help, support, teamwork, and mutual aid. All of these actions should be our goals and conduct practiced, regularly, as husband and wife.

The Scripture above promises us that two are better than one, and their efforts lead to good rewards. The idea presented poses that if one falls, the one can help the other up again. The encouragement is that, in two working together, there will always be a partner to assist. This requires that the two agree on what their relationship paradigm is to consist of. The team can choose to compete and sabotage each other's progress, peace and success or choose to negotiate on a path of compliance and cooperation.

It is much easier for two to lie together and accomplish the generation of warmth than to go it alone. In our marriage covenants, we have promised to aid and abet our spouses in the pursuit of life's many pleasures and challenges. Mutual aid and support is the only way to succeed in being a God-centered, healthy, productive couple. The Scripture goes on to state that although one can be overpowered by attacking forces, two working together can withstand and become victorious.

Today, in your marriage relationship, allow God to be the third strand of the not-easily- broken cord of your life. God, with your cooperation, wants to insure your team effort will be a success that brings glory to Him and that provides fulfilled joy to your heart. Let God be the mediator of your discussions for agreement and planned strategy for marriage and life.

DAY SEVEN
Let God Do the Changing
(Pam)

I Thessalonians 5:11a *(NLT) So encourage one another and build each other up...*

In most of the premarital and marital coaching we do, it amazes me how the theme is so often the same: One spouse wants the other spouse to change. They will sit alongside each other sharing about their situation; and based on the things that are stated, it's very obvious that neither really believes that himself or herself is the problem. I can recall only one woman who called for help and said, "We just need help! If that means that I'm at fault and need to change, I'm willing to do that." It takes a spiritually mature person to say, "Lord change *me*."

When we speak with those who are embarking on the journey of marriage for the first time, we'll ask them, "If any of the things that bother you about your fiancé right now were never going to change, could you live with that?" We ask them that because we want them to realize that getting married is not just another "home-improvement project".

There will always be things about each other that can get under our skin, but it is not our job to change our spouse. Many times, we will criticize, cajole, bribe and even manipulate to try to bring about those changes. Those things may work on children, but adults want the opportunity to make up their own minds on what, if any, changes will be made in them. Even the Holy Spirit, when He deals with us about ourselves and areas in which we may be falling short, always give us the choice of making the changes because of the free will God created in us.

The only assistance God needs from us is to encourage, edify and love unconditionally. Encouragement goes miles longer than any criticism you can think up. Dr. Larry and Judi Keefauver wrote in their book, *Seventy-Seven Irrefutable Truths of Marriage*, "Change always happens from within. Pressure to change that comes from without – a spouse or another person trying to force change – simply doesn't work. Besides when change comes from God's Spirit, the power to grow in that change also comes from God."[1] When you encourage each other's gifts, strengths and talents, you inspire a desire to change because nearly all of us want to be well thought of by our mates.

Let's determine to allow God to do the changing while we become great encouragers and cheerleaders.

DAY EIGHT
Common to Mankind
(Adrian)

1 Corinthians 10:13 *(MSG) No test or temptation that comes your way is beyond the course of what others have had to face. All you need to remember is that God will never let you down; he'll never let you be pushed past your limit; he'll always be there to help you come through it.*

This Scripture should inspire and generate confidence in God and produce a feeling of security for those who trust Him. The promise made here is that no test or temptation we may encounter in life is beyond what is common to mankind, thus assuring us that our enemies will not be able to somehow come against us with a heretofore never revealed weapon of certain destructive power. God has established rules of engagement for both tests and temptations. God will test us to allow us to know what *He* already knows about our commitment to Him but will never tempt us with evil; that's Satan's realm. James 1:13 (NLT) clearly states, "*And remember, when you are being tempted, do not say, 'God is tempting me.' God is never tempted to do wrong, and he never tempts anyone else.*"

    First Corinthians 10:13 also declares that, even when we are tested or tempted, God will not allow anyone or anything to overpower us. This means that God has weighed and measured the events of our life to insure ultimate positive and growth-producing results for all who trust and obey His Word and designed intentions. God's commitment or covenant to His people is that He will never let us down or abandon us, no matter the intensity of the incidents we face. How comforting to hear that God will not permit us to be pushed beyond our limits and will always be there to help us to bear it, endure it, and come through it. Make sure that when life's trials present themselves at your door, you turn to God's promise to always be there for you and to know that He has vetted the situations before they arrive for appropriateness for you and your family.

Life can, and many times does, bring challenges that we do not desire even in our darkest nightmares. Allow these Scriptures to comfort you in knowing that God is protecting you and your family from destructive failure if you can trust Him with your life's journey. No matter what state your marriage relationship or family harmony score is today, you can trust God to bring you through. Just as parents check the temperature and bite size of the food presented to their child, God censors and protects you from devastating, destructive attacks.

Let's not make the mistake of thinking that there will not be test or temptations, but know that they will not overwhelm us due to God's faithfulness. We may not be able to avoid every tough experience, but we have a promise of support and survival from God.

God's plan is one of growth and maturation, so the road traveled with God will always result with the end being better than the beginning!

DAY NINE
Are You Leaving an Inheritance?
(Pam)

Proverb 13:22a *A good man leaves an inheritance to his children's children...*

You may be saying to yourself, "I have no wealth to leave my children or grandchildren." The truth is there are all kinds of inheritances. Children inherit their parent's genes, some personality traits, bad habits, good habits, etc., so I'm not just speaking of money or real estate.

When the above Scripture talks about leaving an inheritance for one's grandchildren, I believe it simply means that what you are passing along is so strong and lasting that it not only transfers to your children but also your grandchildren.

After leaving a heritage of faith in God, one of the greatest things you can leave your children's children is having a fruitful and thriving marriage. When you set the example in front of your children of how to treat one another, how to be faithful, how to honor and respect each other, how to put God first in your relationship, you have set things in motion that will bless your godly seed throughout time into eternity.

God intended for us to carry His presence into every generation after us. It's easy to forget that our lives are not only about us. We are responsible for what we leave behind by way of heritage and legacy. We must weigh everything we do in consideration of how it will affect our children, our children's children and every other seed that follows.

Are you leaving an inheritance? Yes, you are. However, the quality of the type you are leaving is up to you. Let me encourage you to pay attention to what you are doing, saying and living in front of your children. They are! Will it be something worth carrying into the future?

DAY TEN
The Power of Agreement
(Adrian)

Amos 3:3 *Can two walk together, unless they are agreed?*

Matthew 18:19-20 *"Again I say to you that if two of you agree on earth concerning anything that they ask, it will be done for them by My Father in heaven. For where two or three are gathered together in My name, I am there in the midst of them."*

As I view the media's representation of couples and marriage relations, I see how it portrays relationships with unhealthy conflicts and selfish struggles for power or dominance over their mates. People get married for various reasons but one of the primary goals of marriage is a peaceful, joyful, and constructive cohabitation with someone you love and desire to be with.

This thought brings me to Amos 3:3 quoted above. Amos 3:3 asks the question "can two walk together, unless they are agreed?" The answer is a rhetorical no because in order to walk together two must first agree on the direction of travel. Somehow, in our dealings with our spouses, we forget or choose to ignore this very simple fact: In order to travel life's road together, we must agree to agree. One of the greatest deterrents to harmony is pride, and pride derives its origins and strength from selfishness. If we are to have the God type of love in our marriage, it will require the us to act to benefit our mate as the object of our love; that is, the one with whom we have made a commitment to live and partner with the rest of their lives.

Can you imagine a home where the couple is doing their individual best to love, protect, honor, defend, serve, and please the other? A place where selfishness is denied practice, and peace and harmony are pursued as if your lives depended on it. Imagine a home where the plan, purpose, and will of God is priority one.

Now before you turn me completely off, please read the second Scripture above again, Matthew 18:19-20. Remember that God never ask us to do anything that does not require His help with Him being the center of our attention. The blissful existence imagined above is only possible with the help of God. By the very fact that you are married you have two people involved; and if you can desire to agree and ask God to bless your relationship, He promises to be with you in your struggle to possess His promise of peace, joy, and oneness.

The power of agreement is that God promises to grant what the two of you can agree upon in Jesus' name, according to His purpose, and to never leave you alone. If you and your spouse can agree and believe God together, there is nothing that can stand in your way or prevent you from having the will of God for your individual and marriage life. Don't allow Satan or world opinion to fool you into believing that your ability to agree with your spouse is not critically important to the success of your life and marriage.

DAY ELEVEN
Believe the Best
(Adrian)

1 Corinthians 13:7 *bears all things, believes all things, hopes all things, endures all things.*

1 Corinthians 13:7 *(MSG) Always looks for the best, Never looks back, But keeps going to the end.*

1 Corinthians 13:7 *(NLT) Love never gives up, never loses faith, is always hopeful, and endures through every circumstance.*

The world around us seems to foster so much negativity, and if we are not watchful, we will allow it to seep into our homes and marriage relationships. Sometimes, based on our experiences with coworkers, acquaintances, business people, friends, and even family, we can become a little cynical and mistrusting. We'll find ourselves believing and saying that it's hard to trust in people as a general rule.

The Scriptures quoted above from 1 Corinthians 13 are known as the Love Scriptures and define the characteristics of true love in action. I have provided three different translations or paraphrases of the seventh verse with the hope that one, if not all, will resonate with your understanding or bring insight. To be successful in marriage, it is essential that the expression of love be demonstrated by believing the best of our mate. These Scriptures tell us that love always looks for the best, and so should we.

As we live together and come to know each other, we have the opportunity to be familiar with our spouses in a way that few will ever experience. Therefore, we know the times that promises have been made and not kept or forgotten. We can rehearse their mannerism and habits and defend their strengths, also, with pride to those who would try to tear them down. We will stand up for them and, sometimes, even make excuses for them because we love them.

My challenge to you, from the Word of God, is to believe the best of your mate. In the close quarters of marriage there are so many opportunities to offend and be offended, but through forgiveness we have a chance to overcome offences and move forward. Forgiveness affords us the healing from hurts that may otherwise prevent our believing the best. When we don't look back, we have hope for the future and can love our spouses with an enduring love that never gives up.

Give your partner the gift of love that believes the best in them and is willing to have faith to see life through, to the end, at their side.

DAY TWELVE
Cast Your Anxieties
(Adrian)

1 Peter 5:6-9 *(NLT) So humble yourselves under the mighty power of God, and at the right time he will lift you up in honor. Give all your worries and cares to God, for he cares about you. Stay alert! Watch out for your great enemy, the devil. He prowls around like a roaring lion, looking for someone to devour. Stand firm against him, and be strong in your faith. Remember that your Christian brothers and sisters all over the world are going through the same kind of suffering you are.*

Life, with its challenges, presents many opportunities to be confronted and possibly overwhelmed with anxiety. One of Satan's favorite arenas of attack is our family and marriage harmony. Our home life is a situation that is dear to our hearts and can make possessing God's promise of peace and fulfillment seem very distant, if not impossible, to grasp at times. It is wonderful to know that as God has charged us with the assignment to live life according to His plan, He has also given us victory-generating instructions for successful storm navigation in His Word.

Today's Scripture directs us to humble ourselves under the power or into the hands of God. This requires us to admit, and have faith, that God has the solution to our problems and is willing to render aid. God has made it known that He resists the proud but gives grace to those humbled toward Him. The grace, or operational power, of God will result in you being lifted up in honor by God. The same faith that allows you to humble yourself before God will inspire you to throw, cast, or give your cares, worries, and anxieties to God for resolute elimination. Why should we do this, because God has eternally declared that He cares about and for us?

Once you have given your anxieties to God, we are then told to resist our enemy, the devil. In order to resist the enemy, it is necessary that we stay alert to his tactics that cause us to worry and become fearful. Replace your worries with strong confessions of what God has promised in His Word concerning your situation. Fear is the antithesis of faith, and God has declared that He is not the source of fear but of power, love and a sound mind (*2 Timothy 1:7, KJV*). We must stand firm in our belief that God cares and is at work on our behalf, even in the face of fear-creating evidence. God has also promised that the trials we would face would only be those common to mankind with a way to escape guaranteed by God (*1 Corinthians 10:13*).

Follow God's plan for deliverance and manifested victory by giving Him your worries and embracing the peace that faith in God can bring.

DAY THIRTEEN
Be Faith-Filled and Patient
(Adrian)

Hebrews 4:2 *For indeed the gospel was preached to us as well as to them; but the word which they heard did not profit them, not being mixed with faith in those who heard it.*

Hebrews 6:11-12 *And we desire that each one of you show the same diligence to the full assurance of hope until the end, that you do not become sluggish, but imitate those who through faith and patience inherit the promises.*

In 1 Timothy 6:12, the Word of God encourages us to fight the good fight of faith. Within our marriages this is also a very crucial determination and practice for success. Many ask, "Just how do I conduct this battle within my marriage relationship?" The answer is the same as the one for our everyday lives. We undertake this faith fight by first, knowing what we are to believe and are standing upon as promised expectations from God. This is why it is so important that we know, for ourselves, God's will and desire for our marriage and lives as expressed in the Word.

Our battle or struggle is that once we know the promised outcome, to then believe it will be our experience and possession. Faith is the belief that the object of our desires is ours now. This belief today allows us to experience the peace of God that He promised, while the manifestation is realized possibly in the future. Faith, now, in the finished work of God allows us to have hope for the future fulfillment. In our relationships, we have dreams of how marriage should be and are standing on God's Word while waiting for changes in the situation. Faith allows you to walk and behave in love today believing that it is accomplished with hope for the future demonstration either in you or your spouse. This, many times, requires patience on the part of the person waging the faith fight.

Faith requires action now on the part of the person in the faith battle. You cannot wait until the manifestation has occurred to change your position, but you must alter your life, now, with hope for the completed resolution. Hope is based in the actions expected for the future. We must trust God to deliver and know that our adjustment is not based on our spouse but our faith in God, today. To know and have faith in the promises of God is to live committed today with joyful expectation of further fulfillment tomorrow.

Your patience is to be based on your faith in God, resulting in your obedience to His plan today, dependent on His faithfulness not yours or your mate's. The Scripture above reminds us that we may have heard the Word but have not mixed our knowledge with faith. We may have embraced faith but have failed to wait, with patience, for the faithful deliverance of God's promise. Success in marriage and life requires faith for today's obedience with dedicated patience and hope to receive the assured outcome.

DAY FOURTEEN
Identify Your Goliath
(Adrian)

1 Samuel 17:45 *Then David said to the Philistine, "You come to me with a sword, with a spear, and with a javelin. But I come to you in the name of the Lord of hosts, the God of the armies of Israel, whom you have defied."*

Today just might be one of those days when you forget who you are in Christ. We can sometimes become like Saul and the army of Israel when they were facing Goliath on the battlefield and forget that we belong to God Almighty. If you will read 1 Samuel 17, you'll discover that the battle lines between God's people and their enemies had been established for days; and the Israelites refused to confront or address the threat to their peace. Many times, we decide that this is not a battle we can win so we retreat, as we say, "to fight another day".

But God always has a way of reminding us of His promise to never leave us or forsake us.

Just as we may face challenges personally, in our marriages, families, or on our jobs that look overwhelming, remember you are not alone; and God has declared you to be a victor in the arena of life through Jesus Christ. In the Scripture above, Goliath is described as having many weapons of destruction as he came out to face David. The situations of our lives can appear to be insurmountable, but we need to be like David and identify who our enemy represents.

David recognized that Goliath was not just coming out against him personally but that Goliath had aligned himself in defiance of God Almighty. When we can have confidence in our relationship to God - and remember His promised devotion to us - we can boldly face our greatest adversaries with the assurance that we are not alone in our battle. David's confidence came from knowing that God was for him and was more than capable and willing to establish His will in David's life.

To know God's Word – His will for his people – enables us to identify the Goliath-like conditions and attacks that confront us every day. To be able to know and say that failure, unforgiveness, marital discord, sin, financial need, illness, and lack of peace are conditions that are in defiance of God's will for you, will inspire you to fight with conviction as David did. Many of us look at our struggles as a personal problem instead of a shared life event with the odds stacked in our favor because we name the Lord of Hosts as our God. Know that anyone or anything that defies our God is already defeated!

DAY FIFTEEN
A Look Back, A Look Ahead
(Pam)

Ephesians 5:15-16 *See then that you walk circumspectly, not as fools but as wise, 16. redeeming the time, because the days are evil.*

Time travel is one of the most fascinating subjects to ever be explored in stories, movies, etc., and every author or screen writer who tackles this subject tries to put some new twist on it.

The idea of going back in time, to possibly change some things and give the future a different outcome, is something we all dream about at some point or another. We often rehearse our mistakes, errors in judgment, and missteps, and wish we could go back and undo some of the damage or that we could make a different decision.

Rather than take a trip into the past, I would like you to pretend you could have a conversation with the former, younger you. What would you tell yourself as you were about to enter the place where you were going to exchange marriage vows. What warnings would you give besides, "Run, Forest, run!"? What pitfalls would you caution yourself about? What areas would you congratulate yourself in, knowing you will do a good job there? Obviously, we can't go back in time, but we can certainly look to the future.

Most of us know the right thing to do; but if we are honest, sometimes, we just plain don't want to. And yet, I don't think there is one of us out there who doesn't want to hear God say, "Well done, good and faithful servant." Perhaps, in the past, you have not always done what you should have to be a blessing to your spouse, but it's not too late. With God, it's never too late!

They say that the definition of insanity is always doing the same thing expecting different results. Is it time to make some changes? Is it time to look at your past behavior and ask God for the strength to do better? Along with that, though, feel good about the good you *have* done and keep doing it, looking for ways to improve.

We may not have the capability to physically go back in time, but we actually do go there all the time in our minds. We reminisce about what could have been. We wish we had done this or that. Well, let's stop focusing on wishful thinking and get busy with real life. God so wants us to rely on Him for every area of our lives; and marriage is a BIG area. Let's commit it to Him, knowing that, if we allow Him to, He will make it a beautiful, honoring thing that brings glory to His Kingdom. Let's redeem the time we have *now* and look forward to a brighter future.

DAY SIXTEEN
Love in Deed
(Adrian)

1 John 3:18 *(NLT) Dear children, let's not merely say that we love each other; let us show the truth by our actions.*

A deed was found to mean: anything done, an act. The definition further described a deed to be a notable achievement, feat, exploit and finally an action in general as opposed to words. The Scripture quoted above challenges us to not merely say we love but to demonstrate our true love or affection through actions.

It is sometimes very easy to say to our spouses that we love them; but according to this definition, is what we are doing really expressing true love? To love our mate and family is to perform selfless acts of service and care that benefit them. One of the greatest detriments to marital happiness and stability is the selfishness of one or both of the marriage partners. This happens when one partner in the relationship places a condition or requirement that the other partner must act, first, before he or she will display an act of love. In other words, "Serve me first."

The acts of love that are performed should be out of a response to our love for God first, then we can present it as a visible, tangible display of love for our mate and family. Sometimes we can get confused about whom we actually are responsible to for living lives of demonstrated love. The confusion comes when we begin to measure and ration our behaviors of love based on the responses or actions of others to us. The Scripture instructs us to love in deed and not merely word to please God, not ourselves.

We often forget that the plan and processes of God require us to obey Him first in order to enjoy the promises declared in His Word. The love we desire to be shown by our mates may be delayed by our own stubborn refusal to act lovingly. Be determined to show love through actions even when faced with resistance from your spouse. Scriptures tell us that God is Love. Let God work through your actions to bring His victory to completion in you, your marriage, and your family.

DAY SEVENTEEN
Becoming One
(Adrian)

Matthew 19:4-6 *(NLT) "Haven't you read the Scriptures?" Jesus replied. "They record that from the beginning 'God made them male and female.'" And he said, "'This explains why a man leaves his father and mother and is joined to his wife, and the two are united into one.' Since they are no longer two but one, let no one split apart what God has joined together."*

Jesus, in this Scripture, was responding to a question regarding marriage. Jesus declared that through the process of marriage a man and a woman become joined to each other, and the two are united into one. This was, and I believe still is, God's plan for the institution of marriage. God's desire was that no one split apart those who are no longer two but one in His eyes.

What does it mean to become one? I believe that it means the same for the married couple as it does for us to be joined and made one with Christ and God, the Father. Jesus prayed that we would be made one just as He and the Father were one. To be made one is to have love and the same purpose and goals for each other; to desire to see the object of our love blessed, favored by you, protected, and secured. To become one with God is to realize that He has a purpose and a plan for our lives and to be invested in the pursuit and compliant manifestation of His will.

In our Christian marriages, we must believe that God has a plan for each participant that will not destroy or corrupt the plan that God had for the individuals. God created marriage to be a blessing, that is, a good thing for man. When I say man I mean mankind defined as both the woman and the man. A God-centered relationship must respect the plans God had for both parties. What this means is that spouses must communicate to understand the life goals and assignments provided to each of them by God. Once understood, the two who have become one must endeavor to work together to assist each other to accomplish God's call on both their lives as one.

To become one is to believe that God has brought you together to allow you to serve Him better together than you can apart. It is to believe that, as you have become one with Him, His plan will allow you each to be fulfilled and satisfied not only with God but your life mate. Becoming one will require you to unselfishly love and respect the gifts and destiny ordained by God for each of you, and seek His direction for the providence manifested through your unity. As you pursue oneness with God, God will solidify your oneness with each other. God has an ordained plan and destiny for you and your marriage.

Imagine with me, for just a moment, God telling Adam in the Garden of Eden, that after experiencing alone time with God, it was not good for man to be alone; then God introduced His solution to Adam's aloneness in the person of Eve as his mate. God's intention for your marriage is to do us good. Dare to become one with God and your mate, and believe God to deliver goodness to all involved.

DAY EIGHTEEN
The Gift of Change
(Pam)

Galatians 6:15 *It doesn't make any difference now whether we have been circumcised or not. What counts is whether we really have been changed into new and different people.*

I heard a great quote once: "A person won't change until the pain of staying the same is more painful than the pain of change." Another one is, "Insanity is defined as doing the same thing again and again, expecting different results."

If we want something different in our lives, we are going to have to relent to the fact that we must change the way we do some things. Change does not come easily, but it's a necessary part of life; and adjustments must be made from time to time.

In terms of marriage, our relationships will go through many changes and it's important to pay attention to them in order to grow with each other and not grow apart. We must continue to pursue the aspiration to know and understand our partners because they are constantly growing and changing. What we thought we knew about our mate last year may be different this year because he/she has grown in knowledge and wisdom. The older we get, the more we see the world through different eyes. It's necessary to keep our eyes on each other as we progress in our marriages and stay current with the changes that take place in each other.

All too often, we fear change because it may cause us to feel insecure about our future. Our very wise pastor reminded us on Sunday that we cannot expect to go back to an earlier time; neither can we expect things to stay the same as they currently are. Change is inevitable.

As we grow in our relationship with God, we will change for the better, not because *He* changes (Malachi 3:6, "I am the Lord and I do not change"), but because our understanding of Him changes. As we seek His face and draw closer to Him, He reveals more and more of Himself to us. That is a glorious thing! The more we know about God, the more we desire to change into the image of His Son. We must let those changes affect our marital relationships in positive way.

It's important to see change as a gift and not be resistant to it or fearful of it. Things around us will change whether we want them to or not, so let's embrace it, flow with it and change as well.

DAY NINETEEN
Trust That Your Prayers are Being Heard!
(Pam)

Psalm 5:1-3 *(NLT) O LORD, HEAR ME AS I PRAY; pay attention to my groaning. Listen to my cry for help, my King and my God, for I pray to no one but you. Listen to my voice in the morning, LORD. Each morning I bring my requests to you and wait expectantly.*

There seems to be a common thread in many of the chats we have with different couples and individuals when they desire coaching or counseling. After sharing their challenges with us, it becomes very obvious that, although they say they have prayed about a particular situation, they don't really trust that their prayers are going to be answered.

Why is it that we allow ourselves to go through the task of praying; but as soon as we leave our prayer closet, we go right back to worrying and fretting? Are we just practicing some sort of religious ritual with no real expectation of results? Shame on us!

Notice the end of this Scripture selection. David said that he will bring his requests to God and wait expectantly. In the King James Version, it states, "Oh Lord; in the morning will I direct my prayer unto thee, and will look up." It's one of my favorite passages of Scripture because it's so clear that here is someone who trusts that his prayer is being heard and therefore, he is willing to wait with anticipation for the answer.

In Hebrews, the author tells us that "without faith it is impossible to please God" (Heb. 11:6). We can pray and pray and pray some more, but if we don't really believe God is going to deliver, why even bother. It's just an exercise in futility, and it's not pleasing to God. God is moved by faith, not pity.

You may be going through a really tough situation in your marriage or life, in general. God desires to fix the brokenness, but you must believe that He can. Cry out to God for help and then look up because you have faith that He will answer your prayers. Do not nullify your prayers due to unbelief and worry. Have confidence that God has heard you, and you will receive the answers you so crave.

DAY TWENTY
Embrace His Presence
(Adrian)

Exodus 33:14-15 And He said, "My Presence will go with you, and I will give you rest." Then he said to Him, "If Your Presence does not go with us, do not bring us up from here.

Moses had been given direction and purpose as the leader of the children of Israel on their journey to the Promised Land. Moses, in a conversation with God, was promised that the presence of God would go with him. Not only did God assure Moses of His presence but reiterated that rest would be given to the Israelites in the process. Moses' response was to request from God that, "If you don't accompany us, then don't move us." Moses appreciated and acknowledged the importance of the involvement and presence of God in accomplishing the God-given assignment.

Marriage is an institution that was established and is still sanctioned by God. A truly successful marital relationship must embrace the necessity for God's presence and involvement. Just as Moses asked God to go with them, we must do the same for our marriages.

To embrace the need for God's intervention is to recognize that the designed purpose for marriage was to provide help in life and to pursue pleasing Him.

God wants to reveal His love and nurturing character within the marriage relationship. This will require the assistance of God to enable us to successfully demonstrate and share the love we received from Him. God is always giving us examples of love in action because He knows we cannot share what we have not received. Therefore, in order to execute God's plan of unconditional, redemptive love, He must be at the center of our life experience.

The more you involve God, the more you begin to understand that He desires and loves to be invited into every aspect of your life. Marriage is an experience that is no exception. You will find that marriage is not a take home test where you are on your own. God has promised to always be there. Trust Him to be faithful to you and His word. Remember Hebrews 13:5: *Let your* conduct *be* without covetousness; *be* content with such things as you have. For He Himself has said, "I will never leave you nor forsake you."

DAY TWENTY-ONE

Speak Truth
(Adrian)

Ephesians 4:25 *Therefore, putting away lying, "Let each one of you speak truth with his neighbor," for we are members of one another.*

As we read this Scripture, it seems obvious that we should not lie to one another. The verse speaks of being truthful with our neighbor in the body of Christ because we are members of one another. I can think of no closer adult relationship than spouses in a godly marriage; yet, even in our marriages, we are tempted to color or hedge on speaking the truth with our marriage partner.

This situation sometimes arises due to a desire to shield or protect our mates from pain and even pain that might be inflicted on us. As I researched this subject of pain, I saw the definition of hurt as meaning to inflict pain. I also understood the meaning of harm as causing damage; so, in our relationships with our spouses, we say that we don't want to hurt them by being honest or blatantly truthful. However, I believe our true desire should be to avoid doing long-term harm to them or ourselves.

My example is that of a doctor conducting an examination where it may cause pain or even be described as hurting you at the moment. I think that we would all agree that the examination or ensuing procedure, though painful, was not intended to cause ultimate harm. In the same way we must be willing to, perhaps, cause some immediate pain in order to prevent sustained relationship harm. You may ask how you do that? By always speaking the truth in love.

1 Corinthians 13:4-7 *(NLT) Love is patient and kind. Love is not jealous or boastful or proud or rude. It does not demand its own way. It is not irritable, and it keeps no record of being wronged. It does not rejoice about injustice but rejoices whenever the truth wins out. Love never gives up, never loses faith, is always hopeful, and endures through every circumstance.*

Our entire relationship with our spouse must be enveloped in love. We must never be cruel in our expression of truth but remember that today's pain may avert a devastating harm in the future. You may say that you will just avoid the entire subject or continue to speak half-truths. The problem is that you know you are not being completely honest, and, eventually, it leads to anger, bitterness and possibly hatred.

Choose to speak the truth in love, being willing to embrace the hurt of disclosure to avoid the destructive harm of living a lie.

DAY TWENTY-TWO
Generosity Begins at Home
(Adrian)

Proverbs 11:25 *The generous soul will be made rich, And he who waters will also be watered himself.*

Luke 6:38 *Give, and it will be given to you: good measure, pressed down, shaken together, and running over will be put into your bosom. For with the same measure that you use, it will be measured back to you."*

The word generous speaks of someone who is kind, liberal, noble, and substantial in their dealings with others with demonstrated character. Proverbs 11 above indicates that the generous person will be enriched and made to prosper. The concept continues and conveys that this kind or unselfish person who waters or enriches others will also be enriched himself or herself. The Luke 6 Scripture, which is a quote from Jesus, provides even greater motivation by promising us that if we give it will be given back to us in good measure. Some may ask what a good measure is? Jesus left that determination up to us, but qualified the size of the return to be portioned to the gauge we use for our giving.

These are not unfamiliar Scriptures or concepts to many of us as they are frequently used in reference to monetary gifts and offerings. I want to expand and challenge your thinking to extend these scriptural principles to include your conduct and treatment of your spouse, family and individuals with whom God allows you to interact in the process of life. If we commit to being generous in our behavior, first toward our spouse and family, we will have the perfect, safe and controlled environment to practice allowing God to be Lord of our actions and therefore our lives.

God promises in His Word that if we will enrich the lives of our mates, they will in turn do the same for you. Can you imagine having your spouse and children describing your character as being kind, unselfish, and noble in the sense of being worthy of imitation? God says that as you water or nourish and cherish your spouse, they will return the kindness with the result that you will be enriched also. Look at these Scriptures as promises for returns from the surest investment proposed and guaranteed by God. God tells us to be the man or woman He defines in His word, and see if He won't cause others to return to us blessings, pressed down, shaken together, and running over into your heart.

How large of a return do you want to receive in enrichment, blessing, love, kindness, loyalty, appreciation, forgiveness, mercy, and grace? The measure of your gain will be determined by the size of your gift to others. Start your gifting at home and then take it on the road. You will find that God's promises perform anywhere you take them.

DAY TWENTY-THREE
He Knows Our Limitations
(Adrian)

Psalm 103:11-14 *(NLT) For his unfailing love toward those who fear him is as great as the height of the heavens above the earth. He has removed our sins as far from us as the east is from the west. The Lord is like a father to his children, tender and compassionate to those who fear him. For he knows how weak we are; he remembers we are only dust.*

One time, after not having seen or communicated with a particular friend for long time, my wife asked her, innocently, "How have you been doing?" Her response was, "I have been to hell and back since I last saw you". Many of us have faced situations where you may agree with the assessment given by this person. As the conversation continued it was gratifying and encouraging to find out that God had gone with her and brought her safely to her current state of peace and gratitude for His provision through her trying experience.

Some of you may say that your marriage would qualify for the journey described above; but I want to encourage you that if you can trust God with and in your trek, He will bring you out knowing that you are loved unconditionally. Sometimes when we come to ourselves, it is hard to believe that anyone can forgive us, including our spouse or God. God wants you to know that if you can believe His awesome gift of salvation and forgiveness through Jesus Christ, you will experience His forgiveness and establish a foundation for your spouse's forgiveness.

Imagine, if you can, a love based on an intimate knowledge of who you are and every aspect of your life experience and character. God, who knows, desires to see you prosper while compassionately helping you deal with your sins and imperfections. God also knows that once you truly experience His tender love and forgiveness, you will be incapable of not sharing it with your loved ones first and then the world around you.

Share God's love with your spouse and allow him/her to be brought from the hell of failure and defeat to the arms of love that God has gifted you to be for your mate. Allow God to work through you to love your mate while He deals with each of your limitations. Let God bring your marriage to a place of tender and compassionate love, mercy, peace, and grace demonstrated in, on, and through you both.

DAY TWENTY-FOUR
Light Your Home
(Adrian)

John 8:12 *Then Jesus spoke to them again, saying, "I am the light of the world. He who follows Me shall not walk in darkness, but have the light of life."*

Ephesians 5:8-13 *For you were once darkness, but now you are light in the Lord. Live as children of light (for the fruit of the light consists in all goodness, righteousness and truth) and find out what pleases the Lord. Have nothing to do with the fruitless deeds of darkness, but rather expose them. It is shameful even to mention what the disobedient do in secret. But everything exposed by the light becomes visible—and everything that is illuminated becomes a light.*

These verses tell us that Jesus is the light of the world and that we may choose to come out of darkness and walk in the light of Christ. The light that Jesus desires to share with mankind is the light of eternal life which is the God-type of life. Once we have accepted Christ as our Lord and Savior, we emerge from the darkness of a disobedient existence into the light and life of Christ. This life of light is one of goodness, righteousness, and truth. Jesus defined the Word of God as truth.

We are then challenged as followers of Christ to determine or find out what pleases the Lord and expose and eliminate the deeds of darkness. The Scripture goes as far as to say that speaking of the activities of what the disobedient do in secret is shameful. This is where we can begin to bring light into our homes.

As we allow the light and influence of the life and love of Jesus to penetrate the darkness of our lives, we will then be able to shine and illuminate our homes for Christ. It says that everything exposed to the light becomes visible. As you give God permission to expose the darkness in your life and home, the areas of disobedience will be exposed. Dare to consistently expose the darkness to the light of Christ until that darkness becomes light and is transformed into goodness, righteousness, and truth.

The instances of selfishness, disrespect, hatred, lack of loving acts being pursued, jealousy, bitterness, pride, unforgiveness, uncontrolled anger, and on and on must be exposed for what they are by the light within you. Don't hide your areas of darkness, but, boldly, shine the light of Christ on them until they become light. Light your home and see how God will make you and your family become beacons of His light and life, visible to your surrounding world.

TWENTY-FIVE
Drawing a Line in the Sand
(Pam)

James 4:1 *(MSG) Where do you think all these appalling wars and quarrels come from? Do you think they just happen? Think again. They come about because you want your own way, and fight for it deep inside yourselves.*

I watched a movie the other night on the Hallmark Channel. The one nice thing about those movies is that you can almost always count on a happy (albeit possibly unrealistic) ending. This particular story line was about a couple who had decided to divorce. Noticeably, the hallmark (no pun intended) of their current relationship was that they fought constantly, even over silly, minute things. It actually started to get on my nerves because it was so incessant. The sad part about it was that I know there are people who live like that in real life.

If you are a baby boomer, or like watching old cartoons, you will probably be familiar with this line: "That's all I can stands; I can't stands no more!" That was Popeye's famous announcement when he had had his fill of being messed around with by Bluto, his nemesis. He had enough and was going to put an end to it.

At some point, you have got to get to a place where

you draw a line in the sand. It's a line that tells the devil that you have had enough of his interference with your relationship with your spouse – a line that says, "I will no longer allow my selfishness to control my actions, but I will allow the Spirit of God to rule." One couple put it like this: "Despite all the counseling, coaching, and cajoling that was done; the thing that helped us the most was a simple decision. We just decided to stop mistreating each other."

It's so easy to forget that we have the Power of the Universe residing within us – the Holy Spirit. We don't have to fight with human efforts and weapons, anymore. When we decide "that's all we can stands", He is right there to assist us and bring us victory. Draw that line in the sand, and dare the enemy to cross it!

DAY TWENTY-SIX
Aroma or Stench?
(Pam)

2 Corinthians 2:15 *(MSG) Because of Christ, we give off a sweet scent rising to God, which is recognized by those on the way of salvation - an aroma redolent with life.*

Smell is one the strongest senses we have that can create or recreate images. The neighborhood where I grew up was located near the most wonderful family bakeries, and not too far away were commercial bakeries; so the aroma of freshly baked goods filled the air, daily. It was the most delightful experience to walk outside my front door and be engulfed by the unbelievable fragrance of right-out-the-oven bread or chocolate chip cookies.

Several years later, my family moved farther away from the city to the outskirts. Where I could walk to school before, I now had to take a bus. One of the neighborhoods the bus passed was near a slaughterhouse. Gone were the delicious aromas of the goodies I so loved, only to be replaced by the stench of slaughtered cows. Ugh! Fortunately, for me, the memory of that awful smell could quickly be replaced when I walked in the door of our home to find my mom, on her days off, baking one of her famous cakes or pies.

Heavenly!

Think about the words "aroma and stench". Just the sound of them elicits certain images. In defining them, we find that the word *aroma* is a distinctive, pervasive and usually pleasant or savory smell and *stench* is a characteristically repugnant quality or a stink.

According to the above Scripture, being in Christ causes us to give off a sweet scent, one that is pleasing to God. However, I am convinced that if we are not living in obedience to His word, that scent can quickly turn into a stench. And if our marriages are not submitted to God, we are sending out a very unpleasant stink that disappoints our Father and can only be covered by sacrifice provided by Jesus Christ. When others pass by our relationships, are they being drawn in by the perfume of our spirit of agreement, generosity and kindness, or are they being repelled because of the repugnance of our bitterness, wrath, and strife?

Perhaps you feel it's no one else's business what goes on in your marriage, but we must remember that we are not here on this earth just to please ourselves. Paul told Timothy, "...but **be thou an example** of the believers, in word, in conversation, in charity, in spirit, in faith, in purity." (1 Timothy 4:12 KJV) We must live a life that our children can follow as well as other (especially new) believers.

Let's let our marriages be a sweet fragrance of the Life of God in us. It takes work to get there, but we "can do all things through Christ who strengthens" us.

DAY TWENTY-SEVEN
Putting Away Childish Things
(Pam)

I Corinthians 13:11 (NLT) *When I was a child, I spoke and thought and reasoned as a child does. But when I grew up, I put away childish things.*

As we grow in our marriage relationship, God expects us to be mature people and act like adults instead of children. How many times have you wanted to (and maybe even did) say to your mate, "Could you just grow up, already?"

There are many characteristics of a childish person:

A childish person is the center of his own universe.

The mature couple wants to share their lives and makes every effort to make each other feel special and validated.

A childish person can be very insensitive to others.

Maturity causes you to want to be sensitive to your spouse's feelings and make adjustments where necessary.

A childish person is prone to throw a temper tantrum now and then.

Being mature means that you don't allow your temper to run away with you. Remember, the Scripture in Ephesians 4:26 tells us, *And don't sin by letting anger gain control over you.*

A childish person is, at times, non-communitive as a form of punishment.

When you are mature, you realize that the only way to resolve issues is to talk and share your heart.

A childish person will demand his/her own way.

Mature people look for ways to bless their mates and are very willing to acquiesce to the desires of their mates.

My list could go on and on, but suffice it to say that God expects better of us as we grow up. 1 Peter 2:2 (KJV) says, *As newborn babes, desire the sincere milk of the word that you may grow thereby.* We start out as babies and have limited knowledge (and are expected to do so), but as we drink of the Word of God, we will develop into healthy, mature individuals who love our spouses and only want God's very best for them.

DAY TWENTY-EIGHT
Patience
(Adrian)

Romans 15:4 *(NLT) Such things were written in the Scriptures long ago to teach us. And the Scriptures give us hope and encouragement as we wait patiently for God's promises to be fulfilled.*

Hebrews 6:12 *that you do not become sluggish, but imitate those who through faith and patience inherit the promises.*

James 1:4 *But let patience have its perfect work, that you may be perfect and complete, lacking nothing.*

Today we live in a world full of changing and accelerating technology that seems to require and expect ever-faster responses. But today, I was reminded of the need for the personal character quality of patience. It is essential that we exercise patience in all of our relationships in order to demonstrate one of God's many awesome characteristics. It is an extremely important attribute to express in our interactions with our spouse and family to promote harmony and peace within our homes.

In the Romans Scripture quoted above, the word patience is defined as cheerful and hopeful endurance and constancy. If you have lived with or worked with people for very long, you know that staying cheerful and hopeful for extended periods of time can be challenging when left to your own devices. This Scripture gives us hope because it points us to God's Word left for us as instruction to assist us in our patient wait for Him to deliver on the promises He made to us as believers. The Word of God provides examples of those whom have placed their hope and faith in God to answer prayers and strengthen them to follow His will and plan. We must also have faith and be patient with God to come through for our family and us, personally. Trust God enough to extend patience to your loved ones.

The Hebrews verse above encourages us to not become spiritually sluggish, dull or indifferent in our pursuit of receiving God's promises. We are to follow the examples of those who have succeeded, through faith and patience, in receiving God's assurances. Many times, in our patience for God, we must also have patient endurance, forbearance, and fortitude toward our loved ones and friends. To be patient with others is to wait on God to work in their lives as well as ours. The focus of our patience must be on God working in us first, then through us to love others.

James tells us to let patience, or our steadfastness, become fully developed in us. The promise of God is that we will become perfect and complete, or mature in the will, plan, and purpose of God, therefore wanting nothing. What a thought, that as we are patient with God's plan for our lives, we will be able to be steadfastly cheerful and hopeful while awaiting the God-planned developments in the lives of our mates and loved ones. Pursue patience with God's help and gift the patience you've received to others.

DAY TWENTY-NINE
Desires and Expectations
(Adrian)

Psalm 37:3-7 *(NLT) Trust in the Lord and do good. Then you will live safely in the land and prosper. Take delight in the Lord, and he will give you your heart's desires. Commit everything you do to the Lord. Trust him, and he will help you. He will make your innocence radiate like the dawn, and the justice of your cause will shine like the noonday sun. Be still in the presence of the Lord, and wait patiently for him to act. Don't worry about evil people who prosper or fret about their wicked schemes.*

The word desire means to long or hope for something or someone; but it involves the expression of a wish for or a request, while expectation is defined as anticipation, or to look forward to the coming or occurrence of someone or thing. In both our relationships with God and our spouses, there must be an expression of desires or wants for all parties involved in the relationship to understand how to navigate or direct their conduct. God has made His desires known to us in His word which we must study to understand and pursue. In God's Word, he has defined His expectations and defined what we, as His followers, can expect from Him.

In our marriages, we must also take the time to express our desires based upon the desires and expectations we have received from God in His word. I talked in the past about having a plan for your family that is God centered and Word grounded. Making the time to communicate your desires to one another is part of God's plan to manifest the fulfillment of righteousness, peace, and joy in your home. Without expressed desires and the establishment of an agreed family plan, you have a situation designed for disappointment. To have desires uncommunicated with associated expectations is to invite frustration and pain into your family.

God clearly desires and request that we trust, delight, and commit to Him, and rest, or be still in His presence, with patience. God makes these wants clear to us but also declares His desire to assist us in completing everything requested as our partner in life and eternity. God also let us know what we can expect from our commitment to His request. We need to realize that our mates must have the opportunity to understand our desires in order to improve their ability to deliver our requests.

Take time to write down your desires and vision of your relationship separately, and then share them with each other. Agree to discuss each item and over time establish a relationship plan with a promise of commitment.

DAY THIRTY
To Hurt or to Help?
(Pam)

Ephesians 4:2-3 *(NLT) Be humble and gentle. Be patient with each other, making allowance for each other's faults because of your love. Always keep yourselves united in the Holy Spirit, and bind yourselves together with peace*

Think back to your last disagreement with your spouse. Was it resolved adequately? Did you come away from it feeling encouraged or defeated?

When I was first married, I was under the mistaken impression that if you and your mate had a squabble or disagreement, that pronounced the end of the relationship. I have no clue where I got that, but I remember feeling so defeated, not understanding that this was normal. I didn't understand then that these were really opportunities for growth in our marriage.

Since those early years, I can truly look back and see how much stronger our love is for each other as we have learned to take those disagreements and turn them into times to get to know each other a little better. How is that possible? I'm glad you asked.

As we have matured, we understand this: our goal is not to inflict harm on each other, but to help. In other words, neither of us is interested in "winning" the argument, but rather that we really understand each other's feelings and try to alleviate the discomfort. I have confidence going into a disagreement that sharing my feelings with my husband is a safe thing to do because I know that his intention toward me is to bless me. And he knows the same about me. Don't get me wrong; not everything that is said is always pleasant, but our purpose is to gain knowledge and truth, not attack each other. This is not something that happens overnight. It takes love, patience and lots of forgiveness!

So, here is my question to you: When conflicts come, what are your intentions? – to strike a deadly blow so that you win, or is it to help bring some understanding to the situation and get it resolved peaceably? I pray you will do the latter. Trust me; in doing so, both of you come out winners!

DAY THIRTY-ONE
Remain Close
(Pam)

Romans 12:10-12 *(MSG) Be good friends who love deeply; practice playing second fiddle. Don't burn out; keep yourselves fueled and aflame. Be alert servants of the Master, cheerfully expectant. Don't quit in hard times; pray all the harder.*

We have recently relocated to be closer to our family. In the process of our moving and trying to get settled, we seemed to be in frenetic motion. There was always something to purchase, papers to sign, something to clean, something to unpack. In the meantime, both of us were not feeling particularly well physically.

On one of our drives, we noticed a walking trail near our new, temporary residence. It was lush with greenery and very scenic. Adrian made the comment, "We should go back home, take a walk and get reacquainted." The statement took me aback for a quick second. I thought, "What do you mean? We know each other quite well and aren't having any problems." Then I understood what he really meant.

Sometimes, we get so wrapped up in living life that we forget to stop and get reacquainted with the love of our life. It's easy to get so bogged down in the humdrum, boring activities of everyday things that we get comfortable just being on automatic pilot.

This happens all too often in our marriages and also in our relationship with God. These are the two most important relationships we have, and we can't afford to neglect them. We need to be purposely looking for opportunities to connect with and enjoy each other. Intimacy should never grow old or cold, but it does not happen automatically. It must be nurtured and cultivated.

I challenge you to snap out of any stupor you are in and be awakened to the need to stay connected – with your spouse and Our Father God.

DAY THIRTY-TWO
Choosing Your Battles or Don't Push That Button!
(Pam)

Matthew 18:19 *Again I say to you that if two of you agree on earth concerning anything that they ask, it will be done for them by My Father in heaven.*

I Corinthians 13:5b *(AMPC) Love (God's love in us) does not insist on its own rights or its own way, for it is not self-seeking; it is not touchy or fretful or resentful; it takes no account of the evil done to it [it pays no attention to a suffered wrong].*

If you are a normal human being, at some point in your life, you are going to have a conflict with someone: a co-worker, a friend or relative and, of course, your spouse. Unfortunately, it's just the human condition. We all have different ways of doing things; and when others do the things we don't like, we want to let them know and sometimes, not so nicely. It's extremely challenging to always be in agreement with others. We know all the right buttons to push to either keep something going or to shut it down. What if we, deliberately, chose not to push those buttons?

One of the Satan's greatest weapons against married folk is strife. He works overtime to prevent agreement because he knows that is where his power can be decimated! Most couples have no idea of the power at their disposal simply by being in agreement, especially in prayer.

So, it begs the question: Just how important, really, are the things we get in strife about? Think about it. What terrible thing would happen if you decided not to call attention to an offense or not react to it at all? I can hear your wheels turning now, "If I don't say something, they'll do it to me again." That may be true for something serious. However, that is why we need to choose our battles very carefully. Some are important and some simply are not. I remember hearing the story of a man who noticed a piece of paper on the floor under the sofa. He watched it sit there for days and decided that he was going to see just how long it took for his wife to notice it and pick it up. After several days of this, the Holy Spirit whispered gently in his heart, "What is preventing *you* from picking it up?" Shocker! He finally came to his senses and realized that there was no law stating that his wife had to be the one to place that paper in the trash. He finally understood that it was not a battle worth fighting.

We need to save our energies for the things that really do matter so that we can be in agreement more than we are in conflict. Peace is sooo much better! And in an atmosphere of peace, the enemy is defeated on all fronts. Remember, also, that the word clearly says that where there is strife there is confusion and every evil work (James 3:16, KJV)

Let's ask the Holy Spirit to work on our hearts so that we can distinguish the important issues from little irritants. And then, let's ask Him to help us, always, to see our spouses through His eyes and allow our love for them to flourish and keep us in peace and agreement. We know the buttons, but we don't have to push them.

DAY THIRTY-THREE
"Have You Considered My Servant...?"
(Pam)

Job 1:8 *Then the Lord said to Satan, "Have you considered My servant Job, that there is none like him on the earth, a blameless and upright man, one who fears God and shuns evil?"*

What a challenge! God was basically bragging on Job and the kind of man he was. What if it were you or me? Could God brag on us and point us out as an example?

Let's take this to the area of marriage. I started to call this message, "Somebody's Watching You!" because someone always is. But what if God decided to use your marriage as a representative of what a marriage should be or shouldn't be. Which category do you think yours would fall under? It does give you something to think about, huh?

Please don't misunderstand me. There is no perfect marriage just as there are no perfect human beings; but if you are striving to be all God wants you to be and trying to portray a marriage that puts God first in everything, He could very easily put yours on display just because He believes in you.

When God challenged Satan to check out Job, He

described him as "a blameless and upright man who fears God and shuns evil". What struck me most significantly was that once God made those declarations about Job, Satan devised a scheme with the purpose of making God a liar. He (Satan) launched an all-out assault on Job's family, his wealth, his health and his character. When you are serious about God's Word and making your marriage a priority, Satan and his cohorts make it their business to destroy it. However, when you stand fast to the immutable Word of God, just like Job, you will end up the victor.

This trial Job went through showed him what he was made of, and it also revealed some of his shortcomings. Those are not bad things. Sometimes we need to be squeezed to see what comes out of us. When we see the things we don't like, it gives us an opportunity to make the necessary changes and adjustments. This applies to marriage and life, in general.

If you are committed to having the best marriage possible, expect some resistance, but also expect to be victorious as God holds you up as an example for the world to see. Don't give up the fight.

DAY THIRTY-FOUR
A Still Small Voice
(Adrian)

1 Kings 19:11-13 *Then He said, "Go out, and stand on the mountain before the Lord." And behold, the Lord passed by, and a great and strong wind tore into the mountains and broke the rocks in pieces before the Lord, but the Lord was not in the wind; and after the wind an earthquake, but the Lord was not in the earthquake; and after the earthquake a fire, but the Lord was not in the fire; and after the fire a still small voice. So it was, when Elijah heard it, that he wrapped his face in his mantle and went out and stood in the entrance of the cave. Suddenly a voice came to him, and said, "What are you doing here, Elijah?"*

Many times, in our walk with Christ and in our marriage relationship, we find ourselves in a position somewhat like Elijah in 1 Kings 19. Elijah had done his best to be zealous for God but still found himself the object of persecution and hardship. As we navigate our journey of married life, there arise many opportunities to heed the loud voice in our head telling us to run or do something we will regret later.

When we are looking for direction from God or just trying to make the right decision, we need to learn to listen to the still small voice instead of the booming, excited voice. As Elijah was looking to hear from God in his moment of distress, he discovered that God was not communicating in the strong wind, earthquake, or the fire he saw so vividly. But, after all those sensory stimulating events, God presented Himself in a still small voice.

When Elijah had settled his mind and now prepared to listen, God was able to speak to him and asked him "What are you doing here". I believe God is asking many of us the same question after we have yielded ourselves to conduct that is unbecoming of who we say we are and desire to present to our mates and family. Then we ask ourselves, "How did I get into this situation? If we would only listen to the still small voice of the Holy Spirit who always speaks during every condition or situation of life, and choose to follow His directive, we would have greater success at being the person we want to be and God wants us to be.

God has promised to be ever present and available to His people. If you are pursuing God and desire to live His victorious plan for you, listen to the still small voice influenced by God's ever abiding love and character.

DAY THIRTY-FIVE
Trusting My Husband's Wisdom
(Pam)

2 Timothy 3:16-17 *(NLT) All Scripture is inspired by God and is useful to teach us what is true and to make us realize what is wrong in our lives. It straightens us out and teaches us to do what is right. It is God's way of preparing us in every way, fully equipped for every good thing God wants us to do.*

I have learned over the years to trust my husband's wisdom – not easily, mind you. I remember when, early in our marriage, we would disagree on the way something should be done. Fortunately, it didn't happen very often. This one particular time, though, (I don't even remember what the issue was) I wanted to do something one way, and he didn't agree; and I remember asking the Holy Spirit for guidance and also, to help my husband to see things my way. The answer I got back was not quite what I was expecting. He, the Holy Spirit, spoke to my heart, clearly, and told me to trust my husband's wisdom.

Admittedly, when I first heard that, I felt a little annoyed. I mean, I have wisdom, too. Doesn't that count for something? Of course, the more I probed, the more I began to realize that this was not a putdown towards me, but rather, God was giving me some insight into His order of things. There are going to be times when we disagree, but a decision has to be made. Obviously, the best idea for the solution must be sought. It may be mine, it may be his. During those times when both solutions seem viable, we choose his because God has given my husband the responsibility to take the heat for how the family is run.

God has placed our husbands as the head of the home. Submission is one those areas that will be argued by women until the end of time. I, personally, think the reason we balk at it so much is because, deep down (and if we are truly honest), we think we really are smarter than men. We may think, "Why would I, a highly intelligent, strong-minded woman need to be submitted to some man?" But intelligence has nothing to do with God's order. Every person on the earth has to deal with some sort of submission whether it's on the job, in school, the military, government, etc. After the fall, God could have just as easily made the woman the head, but He didn't. I have my own theories about why, but…

The Holy Spirit has helped me to understand, over the years, that when God calls someone to a role or position, He equips them for the task. Therefore, if God has called my husband as the head of my home, certainly, He has equipped him with the wisdom needed to fulfill that role. My part is to trust that that is the case. He may not always get it right, but that's not the point. My ultimate trust is not in my husband but God, who will make sure it all turns out for my good. And because I don't fight my husband on this issue, he has the confidence and motivation to seek God's face in order to make the best decisions possible for our family. He has proven himself to be a very wise leader whom I dearly admire and trust. God bless my Adrian!

DAY THIRTY-SIX
Love Your Own Wife
(Adrian)

Ephesians 5:25, 28-29 *Husbands, love your wives, just as Christ also loved the church and gave Himself for her, So husbands ought to love their own wives as their own bodies; he who loves his wife loves himself. For no one ever hated his own flesh, but nourishes and cherishes it, just as the Lord does the church.*

In these verses, husbands are instructed to love their wives; but it also emphasizes that the wife a husband is to love is his *own* wife. In today's world, that I would describe as over stimulated and exposed, the specification of *own* wife is truly significant and appropriate. People are bombarded with contemporary guidelines for successes that direct us to focus primarily on our own needs and desires above all else. As husbands living in the "me generation", God's Word gives, yet again, another reason to pause and ponder how to actually walk and live the love commanded here.

Husbands are told to love their wives as Christ loved the church and was exemplified in the ultimate act of self-denial and sacrifice. Christ was willing to give up His position in glory to come and die for the object of His love: The Church or Body of Christ. Many of us will say to our wives that we will give our very lives for them but won't take ten minutes to listen to them and provide positive feedback concerning their value to you and your family. Christ's joy was made full, knowing that He had made the way for mankind to be reconciled back to Father God. The cost and sacrifice was indeed counted but given secondary priority to the coveted goal of meeting mankind's greatest need for redemption.

I know we can't die physically every day in demonstration of our love for our wives, but we can make a decision to give them first priority – second only to God, Himself – to love them as your own self or body. This would be awesome to execute for the "me generation". Think about it; all the wonderful dreams of fulfillment and satisfaction we desire for ourselves being shared and targeted with our resources toward our wives. I believe no man in his right mind hates himself but endeavors to be successful and possess a sense of personal wellbeing.

If you love yourself, the best way to bless yourself is to nourish and cherish your wife. To dare to believe that God has established a love plan that benefits both you and your wife. Commit to, selflessly, invest in the growth and development of your wife, knowing that God assures blessings and fulfillment to all involved.

DAY THIRTY-SEVEN
Why Did I Get Married?
(Pam)

Genesis 2:18; 22-24 *(NLT)* *¹⁸ Then the Lord God said, "It is not good for the man to be alone. I will make a helper who is just right for him." ²² Then the Lord God made a woman from the rib, and he brought her to the man. ²³ "At last!" the man exclaimed. "This one is bone from my bone, and flesh from my flesh! She will be called 'woman,' because she was taken from 'man.'" ²⁴ This explains why a man leaves his father and mother and is joined to his wife, and the two are united into one.*

"Why did I get married?" That sounds like a strange question for someone who is very happily married, but I was thinking about it recently. I hear all the time about how girls grow up dreaming about their wedding day. Well, that does not describe me, at all. I never imagined what my gown would look like. I didn't browse through bridal magazines and daydream about all the details that go into a wedding. Quite honestly, I was clueless, which was probably why it didn't bother me to plan my wedding in three weeks and have a tiny little house wedding with my father-in-law performing the ceremony. Actually, my sister-in-law planned it because, as I said, I was clueless.

As I pondered this whole question of why I got

married, it finally dawned on me what images I was formulating, since childhood, in my own heart about marriage. I grew up in the age of "Father Knows Best", and "Ozzie and Harriet", and the like. These programs displayed strong, happy, albeit fictitious, family units where each adult took their proper places. In my house, my father was very dominant and both my parents fought quite often and quite loudly. I knew, by watching those shows, my parents' marriage relationship was NOT the kind of married life I wanted. I wanted peacefulness and kindness and respect and, certainly, love. I didn't realize it then, but I now understand that the Holy Spirit was using those simple little TV programs to shape the image of my marriage today. I realize now that I was much more concerned about marriage than I was about a wedding.

Marriage has been one of the toughest, yet most enjoyable experiences I have had. Sharing my life with my best friend has been the joy of my existence, and I thank God for it.

People get married for different reasons, and based on the many couples we have coached, too many have done it for all the wrong reasons. In fact, in our beginning sessions of pre-marital counseling, one of the first questions we ask is, "Why do you want to be married?" We explain to them that if they are only doing to avoid illicit sex, it's the wrong motive.

God puts people together to accomplish more together for the Kingdom of God than they could apart. He creates the attraction and opportunity for them to fall in love, but then they must capture a vision of their future. It's important to picture yourselves being in love forever and growing old together.

Why did you get married? If it was for all the wrong reasons, take a do-over. I don't mean change partners; I mean reformulate your vision. Ask God to show you the corrective actions to take to get you on the right path to fulfilling your calling as a couple and to help you to experience the love and joy He intended marriage to give.

DAY THIRTY-EIGHT
What Have We Done to Marriage?
(Pam)

I had a conversation with a friend the other day who was going through some difficulties in her life. As I typically do when beginning to coach someone, I asked her to make a list of all the things she would like to accomplish in her life and then prioritize them so she could tackle them with small steps at a time. Interestingly, as she began to verbalize her list, she mentioned marriage and wondered if that was something she really wanted to do someday. She told me, "I don't know if I even really want to get married again. Other than you and your husband, most of the people I know don't seem to even enjoy being married. They barely even like each other. It's like they just tolerate each other. And I'm talking about Christian people!"

That was so discouraging to hear. I know what I observe with my own eyes, and what she stated was true; but just to hear someone else say it out loud made me very sad. What have we done to marriage?! How is it that we have presented it so poorly that unmarried people want no part, and what can we do to change that? It will have to take one marriage at a time.

I want to encourage you to do an assessment of the condition of your marriage. What are its strengths? What are its weaknesses? Actually write them down. Celebrate the strengths! Delight in them, and thank God for them.

Now, about the weaknesses. Remember that list I had my friend make? I urge you to make a list of the things you would like to improve in your marriage. This is something you should do together, and do not allow it to be a time of criticism of each other. Prioritize your items in the order of what you agree to work on first. Making changes in a relationship is hard work, so you must be committed and patient. Your list may be so long that you may feel discouraged, but remember the answer to the question of how you eat an elephant: One bite at a time! Remember also to, "… let patience have its perfect work, that you may be perfect and complete, lacking nothing" (James 1:4,)

As people of God, we cannot be careless or thoughtless in how we live our lives. There are people watching us and making judgments about God based on our behavior. We must never forget Jesus' words in Matthew 5:16, "Let your light so shine before men, that they may see your good works and glorify your Father in heaven." We have a responsibility to show others what a godly marriage is supposed to be.

DAY THIRTY-NINE
Mending Your Funny Bone
(Pam)

Proverbs 17:22 *(NLT) A cheerful heart is good medicine, but a broken spirit saps a person's strength*

When was the last time you and your husband laughed your heads off? Do you realize that the happiest couples are those who know how to laugh together? Some of the most intimate moments shared between couples, other than sexually, are when you can laugh at each other's silly jokes or anecdotes. It draws you together in such a remarkable way, and it helps to strengthen your friendship. Researchers have also confirmed what God's Word already knew: A merry heart and laughter has healing effects on the body.

Sometimes Adrian and I reminisce about comical incidents with our children or even grandchildren, and those memories bring us to tears in laughter. There's nothing like it, and it's so much fun. One of the things we love doing is going out for or sitting down to a cup of coffee to just chat. Usually it's not about anything serious, and most always it's about something funny.

We all know life can be challenging at times, but keeping a sense of humor throughout it is a God-send. Laughter takes the edge off stress and can keep you focused on the goodness of God. When we are able to concentrate on His goodness, our burdens are lightened, and we can see more clearly to a solution.

So, dear ones, my assignment for you this week is to rent some comedy movies, or buy a clean joke book and laugh until you fall into each other's arms. What happens after that is up to you.

DAY FORTY
Custom-Designed Creatures
(Pam)

Psalms 139:14-15 (NLT) *Thank you for making me so wonderfully complex! Your workmanship is marvelous -- and how well I know it. You watched me as I was being formed in utter seclusion, as I was woven together in the dark of the womb.*

Have you ever had anything custom designed? I remember growing up noticing anytime my dad purchased a new car. No matter how many others had the same model, he always asked for a custom color – something no one else had. That made it special to him, and he took such pride in it.

We are God's custom-designed creatures. He is proud of us! He has made us unique in every way. Even twins who share the same DNA have some differences in personality, character, temperament, etc. And because He has made the effort to design us so carefully, we are very special to Him; and we need to appreciate it fully – in ourselves and in others.

Aren't you glad that we are all different? We generally celebrate those difference until we get married, then we want our mates to be just like us and do things just like we do. In other words, we want to change them. God made us different for many reasons. Sometimes, we have rough edges that God uses our mate to help smooth out or soften. Sometimes, He uses them to toughen us up a bit. Proverbs 27:17 says, "As iron sharpens iron, a friend sharpens a friend." Your best friend is (or should be) your spouse. Rubbing up against each other's differences, makes you a better person if you don't resist it. I have heard it said that if I and my husband were just alike, one of us is unnecessary.

Let's give each other the gift of acceptance. When I can tell my mate, "I know that you and I may differ in our approach to life. I know we each have quirks and idiosyncrasies that could drive us up a wall, and I know that I may use my feelings and intuition in problem-solving while you use more logic. I accept you just as you are because that is how God created you. He allowed all your life experiences to shape you into the person you are today. He didn't make a mistake in blending our two lives to make one beautiful life" What a blessing! When we can offer that gift to our husband or wife, the possibilities of joy and fulfillment are endless. When we can do that for each other, we will stop trying to change each other. Instead we will allow the Holy Spirit to do that. That's *His* job, after all, not ours.

DAY FORTY-ONE
Castle or Kingdom
(Adrian)

Romans 14:17 *(ESV) For the kingdom of God is not a matter of eating and drinking but of righteousness and peace and joy in the Holy Spirit.*

Conventional or contemporary thinking would have us believe that our home is our castle. The concept driving this declaration is that with all the societal and governmental intrusion into our personal lives, the only place where you can really exert some semblance of authority is within your home. To many this means that home is the place where you can let down your hair, wear what you want when you want, say what and how you really feel without incurring significant negative consequences. The term "castle" implies that there should be a lord to rule the domain. The Word of God declares there is only one Lord, Jesus Christ.

I want to challenge us all to allow our homes to be a part of the Kingdom of God. Once this has occurred, our homes come under the authority of Jesus Christ and can no longer be a place where anything goes or where rules of Christian conduct are suspended by the decree of its occupants. Those who do not accept the Lordship of Christ in their homes seem to always want to demonstrate love, patience, and forgiveness in the public arena more vigorously than at home. Somehow, their castle and actions become like the commercial for Las Vegas vacations in that "what happens in Vegas stays in Vegas". I want to make you aware of the fact that God should reigns in Vegas and our homes, but some refuse to submit to or pursue His Lordship.

When we refuse to treat our spouses and family members as if we are the charges of God Almighty, we are declaring ourselves to be in some self-defined God-free zone. There should be no zone, region, attitude, or relationship where we are not accountable to God. We cannot turn God's awareness and responsibility to us on and off because we are in our castle. As Christians, we and our castle exist in the Kingdom of God at all times.

Allow your homes to be the place where you practice obeying the will of God for your life and loved ones. Determine to be an example of the Lordship of Christ in your home to your spouse, children, and other family members. If no place else on earth, let your home be a representation of the dominion of God and the influence that He can have on willing and compliant human beings. Choose to live in God's kingdom and not in your self-proclaimed castle. Let Jesus, indeed, be Lord of all your life, and experience the righteousness, peace, and joy promised by God today.

DAY FORTY-TWO
May I Serve You?
(Pam)

Galatians 5:13 *(NLT) For you have been called to live in freedom, my brothers and sisters. But don't use your freedom to satisfy your sinful nature. Instead, use your freedom to serve one another in love.*

Mark 9:35 *(NLT) He sat down, called the twelve disciples over to him, and said, "Whoever wants to be first must take last place and be the servant of everyone else."*

One of my favorite programs to watch was Downton Abbey. If you followed the show at all, you immediately understood that there was a distinct difference between the servants and those whom they served. One thing that particularly stood out for me was that the servants knew that their job was to serve; it's what they had been trained to do and had been part of families who had been doing it for generations. Except for a few exceptions, most didn't seem to resent their positions but, rather, took great pleasure in serving with excellence.

It's unfortunate, but in marriage many have forgotten that we are to be servants of one another. I think most people go into a marital relationship thinking about what they are going to get out of it instead of what they are going to contribute. Imagine what our lives would be like if we woke up every morning with the thought, "How may I serve my spouse today?" The very best servants are those who try to anticipate the needs of someone even before they ask. I'm not suggesting that we become mind readers. What I am suggesting is that we pay attention to our mates and study them to discover where they need help so that we can lessen their loads any way we can. More times than not, it's in the little things we do.

I recently heard a motivational speaker tell of the experience of his first job as a valet for the Ritz-Carlton. He shared that their motto was: "We are ladies and gentlemen serving ladies and gentlemen." He told us that it was stressed that this philosophy was not just for their clientele but amongst the team of workers as well. Sometimes I think it's easier for us to put on a good front as we are out and about in the world, but once we cross the threshold of our homes, we forget to continue to be servants. If anything, this is where we need the most practice. In other words, we need not take each other for granted in this area.

Let's pray that God gives us a servant's heart toward our mates. Let's make ourselves available to each other through serving one another, and let's see who can out serve the other. When we become servants, we become the greatest in God's eyes.

DAY FORTY-THREE
Do What's Right
(Adrian)

1 John 3:18-21 *My little children, let us not love in word or in tongue, but in deed and in truth. And by this we know that we are of the truth, and shall assure our hearts before Him. For if our heart condemns us, God is greater than our heart, and knows all things. Beloved, if our heart does not condemn us, we have confidence toward God.*

My children reminded me recently that one of most memorable statements I always challenged them with was "Always do what you know to be right". Some may ask, "Just what is *right*?" This is a critical question for each individual to answer and pursue for the rest of their lives. When I told them to do what they knew was right, I was actually instructing them to do what they believed in their heart was the right thing to do at that time. We must all understand that our knowledge and comprehension grow and develop just as our physical bodies do. We can only give or respond based on what we have in our possession.

The Scripture quoted above encourages us to love not only in words but also through our actions or deeds. It further states that we are able to really know we are of the truth or in fellowship with God by our actions. It is when we see the effect of how God's presence in our lives has changed us for the good that we can assure our hearts before God. The problem for many of us is that our own hearts condemn or make us feel guilty because of what we see ourselves do. You may ask if we will ever be perfect and the answer is: Not in this earthly life. The hope of our confidence toward God is in believing that Christ has paid for our sins/imperfections and allows us, when we ask for forgiveness, to have a reality and sense of relational restoration with Father God.

It is crucial that we are connected to God through the life and work of Jesus Christ. If we are, then we will have a desire to walk in truth and will make it our life's pursuit to know the will of God and to be found doing what we believe is His will every day. The exciting part of living for God daily is that we are constantly expanding our knowledge and behaviors into the image of Christ. Just know that when you find out tomorrow that what you believed yesterday was not the whole truth, or right, God, who knows everything, is greater than our hearts and has covered us through Christ's finished work.

Always do what you believe is right toward your spouse, family, and mankind, in general. Obey God's commandment to love, and be assured in your heart before God.

DAY FORTY-FOUR
Be Reconciled
(Adrian)

Matthew 5:23-24 *(MSG)*

23-24 "This is how I want you to conduct yourself in these matters. If you enter your place of worship and, about to make an offering, you suddenly remember a grudge a friend has against you, abandon your offering, leave immediately, go to this friend and make things right. Then and only then, come back and work things out with God.

When we are instructed to make things "right", the true meaning of the word originally used was to be thoroughly changed or reconciled. To reconcile means to restore to friendship or harmony. The reality of all our human interactions is that conflict and disharmony often arises. Love, in its perfect state, is a condition of perfect harmony described by many as paradise. When harmony is disrupted, in order to reestablish love, we move into a restorative mode known as reconciliation.

The most intimate relationship a human being will experience as an adult is within the institution of marriage. Those who have been involved in the practice of marriage will attest that conflict has a way of intruding and making, at times, a full display of discord. The desire to live in a state of love, harmony, and peace with our mate prompts us to make an effort to demonstrate our commitment and determination to be reconciled.

Our Scripture today provides added incentive for those desiring to have peace and harmony with God. We are directed to make it right with those whom we, knowingly, have experienced conflict. Only after we have made an attempt to make peace can we then approach God with our gifts for Him. This is how important it is to God that we not let issues fester with people and especially our spouse. I say "especially with our spouse" because you know when discord has occurred and is hovering over our relationship.

God has defined Himself as love; and, therefore, as an individual desiring to express His presence in your life, love should be a trait you exemplify. The challenge with the things God desires to be manifested in our lives is that we cannot consistently and authentically portray His character without His help. The process of being reconciled to anyone cannot be accomplished without a commitment to God and a life filled with love in action. To be reconciled requires releasing our selfish objectives and allowing God to change us into His love, personified.

Don't allow offences, grudges, anger, pride, being right, pain, and self-interest to prevent you from being the source of harmony in your home or anywhere you are. Dare to refuse to accept disharmony when *you* can take steps to bring reconciliation to your sphere of influence. Resolve to believe God to use you to bring more agreement and peace to your world.

DAY FORTY-FIVE
At the Cost of My Sanity?
(Pam)

Psalm 37:4 *(NLT) Take delight in the Lord, and he will give you your heart's desires.*

Some friends of ours had some projects they wanted to accomplish; and while discussing them, the wife had much bigger plans than her husband felt able to accommodate due to cost and scope. He gave it all much thought, fretting over it when he finally made this statement to her, "Sweetheart, you know that I want to please you and give you what you want, but should it be at the cost of my sanity?"

In any healthy marriage relationship, each spouse tries to meet the needs of the other. It's important, however, to keep our desires reasonable and not allow them to become oppressive. Love helps keep us in check. I use to tell people, all the time, that, if I wanted the moon and he could afford it, my husband would try his best to get it for me. Of course, because I love him, I would never request such a ridiculous thing.

What kinds of things are we asking our mates to do? What "needs" do we impose on them that could be construed as unreasonable? Ladies, are we asking our husbands to keep us in a particular lifestyle that the family budget can't really afford? Gentlemen, are you asking your wives to "bring home the bacon" and also "fry it up in the pan"? In other words, are you asking her to work a full-time job and still keep the home clean and in order by herself?

It's important to distinguish between wants and genuine needs. Everyone's needs are different, so I can't specifically define that distinction for you. You have to do that, together, as a couple. One of the special things that happens in a healthy relationship is, because you are both working towards meeting each other's needs, you will both work towards also trying to provide some of the wants. Our verse above tells us that as we delight ourselves in God, He gives us the desires of our heart. I believe, also, that it works that way in a marriage. As we delight in meeting the needs of our mates, they will seek out the desires we have and try to fulfill them.

The best protection of each other's sanity is by fulfilling the command in Matthew 7:12 (Message): "Here is a simple, rule-of-thumb guide for behavior: Ask yourself what you want people to do for you, then grab the initiative and do it for *them*. Add up God's Law and Prophets and this is what you get." A simple, yet profound, truth to live by.

DAY FORTY-SIX
Going Down Deep
(Adrian)

Ephesians 3:17-18 *(NLT) And I pray that Christ will be more and more at home in your hearts as you trust in him. May your roots go down deep into the soil of God's marvelous love. And may you have the power to understand, as all God's people should, how wide, how long, how high, and how deep his love really is. May you experience the love of Christ, though it is so great you will never fully understand it. Then you will be filled with the fullness of life and power that comes from God.*

Most of us don't have a clue just how much God really loves us. We think that we can increase His love for us by the good things we do; and in that same vein, we think we lose God's love by the bad things we do. If we have accepted Jesus' substitutional death, then His love for us is settled! Certainly, there is growth that is needed by us, but that doesn't change or diminish God's love for us in any way. We just need to live out that knowledge.

The Scripture above gives us comfort in knowing that, when we truly experience the love of Christ, we will enjoy full life and power. Jesus said that He came to give us abundant life! That means a life full of victory.

How is this translated to marriage? Marriage is one

of those areas where the enemy has convinced many people that it is nearly impossible to be truly happy. I believe that is because so many of us have not tapped into the power of God that causes us to be successful. If the Spirit of God lives in me, then I have the power to treat my spouse with kindness, respect, forgiveness, and deep love. Think about how you feel when you not only know that you are loved but actually *feel* loved. It changes your whole outlook! You treat others better because you feel better about yourself.

As Paul has said, we may never fully understand the depth of the love of God towards us, but we can sure experience it. I encourage you to meditate on it, let it fill your heart, and then share it with your mate. I guarantee that your marriage will change to such extent that all others around you will want what you have because you will be living the Word in their presence. Everyone wants to believe that the Word of God is true – they just haven't seen it to be so in enough lives. Why not demonstrate the truth of God's Word in your life and marriage? Go down deep into the soil of God's love!

DAY FORTY-SEVEN
Friends
(Adrian)

John 15:13 *Greater love has no one than this, than to lay down one's life for his friends.*

This Scripture is a quote from Jesus as He talks about His love and the extent that love causes people to go to in expression or demonstration of their love. As I researched the meaning of friend in the dictionary I found the following definition: *a person whom one knows and with whom one has a bond of mutual affection, typically exclusive of sexual or family relations* (New Oxford American Dictionary). I challenge you to make friends with your spouse and allow them to become, if not your best friend, at least named among the best. There ought to be a mutual bond of affection that goes beyond sexual attraction, and is attachment-based and not function-based.

Your mate can be a friend that is a supporter of your cause and in whom you find commonness of purpose, goals and cause. Your spouse should not be an enemy but the special someone who's on your side because they know your heart. This may involve some giving of your life in expression or demonstration of your love. Fortunately, I am not talking about physical death but possible sacrifice of life's personal treats and attractions. We are often quick to say that we would give our lives for our mates and family but will not sacrifice our personal time to meet the need or desire of each other.

How wonderful it is to know that there is someone who is rooting for you and wants to see you succeed even if it means they come in second; to have a friend with whom you desire to spend time, expend energy and resources to assure their comfort and fulfillment in this life; a person to whom you are attached, not because of what they can do for you but because you have spent the time to know them intimately. And, having come to know them intimately, you are affectionately bonded to them no matter what anyone else says or does.

God created us for His glory and personal fellowship. In our marriage relationship, we have the opportunity to truly get to know another human being on a level only exceeded by our relationship to God. Dare to pursue your mate as your dearest and best friend. Allow yourself the pleasure of being loved for whom you really are and not the image packaged and prepared for public consumption. Give your spouse the life-long opportunity to be affectionately bonded to you.

DAY FORTY-EIGHT
Growing Old Together
(Pam)

Job 12:12 *Wisdom belongs to the aged, and understanding to the old.*

Isaiah 46:4 *I will be your God throughout your lifetime—until your hair is white with age. I made you, and I will care for you. I will carry you along and save you.*

We live in a day and age where youth and beauty are celebrated as never before. Think about all the beauty products that are out there trying to erase the years. It's almost dizzying going to a cosmetics counter with all the choices available, not to mention all the things you can purchase online. There are medical procedures that can lift your breasts, insert extra padding in your bottoms and remove that excess fat around your mid-section. We are terrified of getting old! But we shouldn't be.

With age comes wisdom. Admittedly, there are some very immature old people, but God's plan is that as we grow, we grow in wisdom. Couples who allow themselves to grow old together know a secret that the young don't: Love takes time and encompasses every aspect of your being.

One of the saddest things about divorce is that

some couples will never get to experience the joy seeing their love mature with the same person. And one of the saddest things most young people don't recognize is that they don't fully grasp or understand the depth of true love that can only be developed over time. It's when you go through the trenches together over many years that you make wonderful discoveries about life, love and your mate. One unknown author said this: "True love isn't Romeo and Juliet who died together. It's grandma and grandpa growing old together."

Growing old can be a bit scary, especially, to the very young, and sometimes, we have to work hard at embracing the aging process. Having a partner to share it with makes it more tenable, though.

How many times have you seen older couples strolling down a path holding hands. Nearly everyone has the same reaction, "Isn't that sweet" or "How cute." It is, indeed, sweet and it can only be experienced through a lifetime of shared loving and caring.

DAY FORTY-NINE
Stuck Like Glue
(Adrian)

People often say to my wife and I that when they see one of us the other is almost always nearby. They have accused us of being joined at the hip or stuck together like glue. Of course, we are not actually attached physically, but we do believe in and diligently pursue being joined in purpose and love for God. The image and reality of our togetherness has come from years of determination to allow God's plans to be ours. We have chosen to let God be our source of peace, joy, and fulfillment by believing that our union is part of God's grand strategy to bring contentment to both our lives. We are a husband and wife desperately in love with God and submitted to becoming one flesh in Christ.

Genesis 2:24 *Therefore a man shall leave his father and mother and be joined to his wife, and they shall become one flesh.*

Looking at the definition of one and flesh from the original Hebrew, it gives us the meaning of "united person". God intended for the couple joined in the union of marriage to become a united person. This union would require them, husband and wife, to reorder the priority of father, mother, personal family bonds, and even self beneath that of the one-flesh bond to their spouse.

Society would have us fight for our individuality over the existence of the God-given, one-flesh model for our marriages. The union that grows from marriage must create an "us" that may be very different in some ways from the "you and I" who entered the union. This union development, if orchestrated by God, will not be destructive to any godly plans and character qualities intended for the individual by God. The process of loving and coming to know one another for the purpose of blessing each other is God's design. God's intention was to make our lives even more blessed and fruitful by providing adaptive, completing, and helping mates for us to serve Him better in spiritual unity with God.

God's love was manifested in the creation of the institution of marriage for Adam and Eve, and ultimately you and I. The advancement and protection of the union of marriage was to be superseded only by the development and defense of our relationship to God. For you see, the love we experience from God is the foundation and format for the loving affection and devotion to be practiced in our marriages. God-centered marriages will be focused on loving and serving each other to the degree we have received love from God and desired to serve Him.

Allow God to be the glue that sticks you and your mate together in unity. Make the personal choice to let God's love for your spouse be personally confirmed through you, joined by choice in order to be positioned to receive God's blessing of a "united- person" marriage.

DAY FIFTY
The Gift of Acceptance
(Adrian)

Acts 10:34-35 *Then Peter opened his mouth and said: "In truth I perceive that God shows no partiality. But in every nation whoever fears Him and works righteousness is accepted by Him.*

God has made provision for mankind to be accepted in the family of God through the life, death, and resurrection of Jesus Christ, according to Ephesians 1:6. The word used for accepted in this Scripture speaks of being encompassed with favor and to honor with blessings. In other words, God has declared those who have received His Son as Lord and Savior to be highly favored and accepted, in His estimation. This is great news to those born again into the family of God and something you need to experience as a child of God.

It is my belief that God intends for us to share the blessings and experiences we have received from Him with our fellowman. I believe that we cannot give what we have not received; and therefore, just as with forgiveness, acceptance is to be shared with those who cross our life's path. We must realize true love, forgiveness, and acceptance originates and exudes from God alone. How wonderful to know that I am not only forgiven by God but I am accepted by Him.

In our marriage, we sometimes express our love for one another but withhold our acceptance. We may, jokingly, say that we love each other, warts and all, and in fact, we should. The emphasis here is that the warts may be what makes your mate who they are, and we need to truly learn to embrace them. We should celebrate our uniqueness through acceptance, expressed by surrounding them with favor and love. Our mates need to know that someone appreciates the true essence of who they are – desiring to be in their presence and determined to make an extraordinary effort to know, understand, and appreciate the individuality embodied in them.

Our marriage atmosphere should be a place of acceptance and not just tolerance. If you have received the love, forgiveness, and acceptance of God through Christ, then petition God to help you share and exemplify that divine character with your spouse. Make it your life's goal to be an imitator of Christ every day and everywhere.

Share the gift of acceptance with your spouse and create an environment where God is tangibly gloried and acknowledged.

DAY FIFTY-ONE
Be On Guard
(Adrian)

1 Corinthians 16:13-14 *Watch, stand fast in the faith, be brave, be strong. Let all that you do be done with love.*

It has been my experience, and I believe it to be true for many of us, that the world and its imposing events, situations, and circumstances appear to be happening at a break-neck pace. Technology that is advertised as time-saving tools have instead become time thieves with their own list of demands and commitments. Our lives seem to be pulled in diverging directions with conflicting priorities that promote confusion and uncomfortable instability. This appears to be the age we live in, but we don't have to be conforming participants. We can and must discover, through God's help and direction, the joy, peace, and fulfillment-producing priorities meant for those who trust in and rely on His faithfulness.

    The Scripture quoted above spoke volumes to me regarding the condition of most of our lives and family. The first directive was to watch or be on guard. What are we to be watching for? Watch and be on guard for the tactics of our world system and Satan who distract us from the plan and purpose of God for our lives. Satan's main strategy is to cause us to question the intent, capability and character of God and His will for us. These attacks come in the form of offences where our expectations are misguided, disappointed, or delayed. We must always be on guard not to place our desires and plans above God's because only the will of God will survive the test of life and time.

We need to stand strong in our faith in God to deliver what He has promised at exactly the right time and place; that is, stand in the sense that you are immoveable even in the face of lying evidence. Lying evidence would cause us to believe that the thunderstorms of life will never pass and that the morning is only a distant memory, never to be experienced in the manifesting fact of a gloomy night. We must be brave and strong to hold to our professions toward God and confessions of His integrity and reliability while we look and strain to see the sun rise at its appointed time in our life.

As you trust and wait with patience for your daily bread and deliverance, look for chances to demonstrate the love of God. Start in your home with your spouse, children, family, and friends. Then let the world see that everything you do under the influence of Christ is done with love. Be on guard for occasions of charity to be performed, i.e. love in action. Use your faith to be a brave, strong, lover of God, and thereby a lover of your neighbor.

DAY FIFTY-TWO
How Close?
(Adrian)

Genesis 2:23-24 *And Adam said: "This is now bone of my bones and flesh of my flesh; She shall be called Woman, Because she was taken out of Man." Therefore a man shall leave his father and mother and be joined to his wife, and they shall become one flesh.*

Today I had the opportunity to speak to a young man who was planning to be joined in marriage next month. I was talking to him about the importance of making time to listen to God and, ultimately, obey His directions. The thought was that no matter how much he thought he loved his fiancée at this moment, his love and knowledge of her would grow. Their love would grow to a place that, even when faced with vigorous testimony from someone else regarding a misdeed, he would trust his knowledge of her over their accusation.

This state of love or confidence in your mate does not occur just because you say, "I do" at the marriage altar. This place of knowing and experiencing the heartfelt belief in the character, intent, and deliberate actions of your mate result from time and space shared in the passage of time. It occurs because you have made a deliberate choice to love, get to know, and experience your mate over time.

The Scripture above speaks of a person leaving parents and being joined to his or her spouse as an act of their will. The parents and family represent the familiar and, sometimes, comfortable relationships of the past. The question posed in this devotion is "How Close?" How close do you desire to become with your spouse? Scripture defines the goal of marriage as becoming one flesh – one in heart, purpose, goal, and direction. This will only happen when you decide to get close enough to your spouse to be able to hear their heart beat. Close enough to realize that your joys and hurts are shared and affect both of you.

Ephesians 5:29 *For no one ever hated his own flesh, but nourishes and cherishes it, just as the Lord does the church.*

We must get close enough to our mates that we view them as our own flesh and would never do anything to harm them or ourselves – close enough that married life truly means sharing everything until you strengthen each other and demonstrate love as one entity.

DAY FIFTY-THREE
Bringing the Fire Back
(Pam)

Revelations 2:5 *(NLT) Look how far you have fallen from your first love! Turn back to me again and work as you did at first.*

One of the greatest joys in my life is a roaring fire in a fireplace. It's a simple pleasure that makes me feel loved and special.

Think about a wood-burning fireplace. You have to place the wood on the grate, put a little kindling underneath it, perhaps even a bit of fuel; then you light it. With a bit of coaxing and stoking, the flames burst forth. Once it gets going fully, you have a beautiful fire. You're enjoying it; it's warm and cozy and wonderful! After a while, you notice the flames are barely flickering. You make a decision at that point. Do you let the fire die down to the point of leaving only burning embers, or do you attend to the fire by adding more wood to bring it back to a blaze?

Marriage is much like that fire. When we first get married, we are ablaze with passion for each other – not just sexually – but in our care of each other. We want to do everything we can to please one another. Over time, however, our fire dies down, and we are left with burning embers. The good thing about embers, though, is that we can easily stir things up again and get the flame back. The problem comes when we have neglected the fire for so long, the embers, themselves, have gone completely cold and no amount of stirring or stoking can bring them back.

The solution: Start a new fire! How? Go back to the early stages of your relationship and remind yourselves why you fell in love. Talk about the things that excited you about each other. Do your own version of Elizabeth Barret Browning's poem, "How Do I Love Thee." The poem goes on to say, "Let me count the ways." You will be amazed how that will affect you. Then begin to take time every day to reconnect. Make the decision to never again let your love grow cold. It will always be your choice.

DAY FIFTY-FOUR
Be Persistent
(Adrian)

Mark 8:22-25 *(NLT) When they arrived at Bethsaida, some people brought a blind man to Jesus, and they begged him to touch the man and heal him. Jesus took the blind man by the hand and led him out of the village. Then, spitting on the man's eyes, he laid his hands on him and asked, "Can you see anything now?" The man looked around. "Yes," he said, "I see people, but I can't see them very clearly. They look like trees walking around." Then Jesus placed his hands on the man's eyes again, and his eyes were opened. His sight was completely restored, and he could see everything clearly.*

Many times, in life, we face resistance or opposition to our plans and pursuits. We find this to be the way of life where we must learn to sail not only with favorable winds but also against opposing winds in order to reach the desired destination. Our marriage relationships are a part of life that sometimes seems to be overrun with opportunities for conflict and disagreement, but I want to encourage you to be persistent in your pursuit of harmony.

Today's Scripture speaks of townspeople who had brought their request to Jesus, desiring that He heal their blind friend. Imagine the boldness and high expectation of the community to see a miracle performed, not to mention the blind man's own anticipation. Jesus, being the representative of His Father's love and desire to meet humanity's needs, agreed to minister to the man. Sometimes, in our lives, we find that not everything comes out exactly as we aspired after the first encounter. Here Jesus ministers to the blind man and then asked him how well he saw. The man's response was that his eyesight was better than before but still not all that was expected. Have you ever had an experience like this in your life and what did you do?

In the story, we find that Jesus laid His hands on the man again with the result that now the once blind man's eyes were completely restored. Many of us give up on the relational situations in our marriages after having confronted them once or maybe numerous times. But, when you believe that God hears and is willing to assist and minister healing to your personal situation, you will be willing to address the issue again, remembering always to wait on God's best to ultimately be delivered. In the above instance, the persistence in prayer was rewarded with full restoration and affirmation of God's true intention.

We must be persistent in our belief in God's determination to be a promise-keeping, faithful deliverer of those who stand or wait in faith. Don't be discouraged when your first or third approach to God's plan for your life meets resistance. Persist in the pursuit of God's plan of marital harmony and satisfaction. Understand that it is God's plan that will produce the greatest blessing and life satisfaction.

DAY FIFTY-FIVE
Only One Standard
(Pam)

1 Corinthians 13: 4-8 *(AMPC) Love endures long and is patient and kind; love never is envious nor boils over with jealousy, is not boastful or vainglorious, does not display itself haughtily. It is not conceited (arrogant and inflated with pride); it is not rude (unmannerly) and does not act unbecomingly. Love (God's love in us) does not insist on its own rights or its own way, for it is not self-seeking; it is not touchy or fretful or resentful; it takes no account of the evil done to it [it pays no attention to a suffered wrong]. It does not rejoice at injustice and unrighteousness, but rejoices when right and truth prevail. Love bears up under anything and everything that comes, is ever ready to believe the best of every person, its hopes are fadeless under all circumstances, and it endures everything [without weakening]. Love never fails [never fades out or becomes obsolete or comes to an end].*

There are very few people who can honestly say that the above Scriptures describe their love walk to a tee. It's a very high standard, but God's Word is the only standard by which we can compare ourselves.

How often have you found yourself comparing your marriage to someone else's? That knife cuts both ways. We may see a couple who is less off than we are and begin to feel pretty good about how we are performing. Or we may observe another couple who always seem to be doing everything right, and, thus, we condemn ourselves because we don't feel we measure up. Either situation is problematic because we are forgetting what the true standard is.

God's Word is our measuring stick. Our goal should be to strive to live according His Word and see progress regularly. According to Dr. Larry and Judi Keefauver's book, *Seventy-Seven Irrefutable Truths of Marriage*, the standard includes these components: unconditional love (agape), servant attitude and lifestyle, sacrificial friendship, and honoring and esteeming your mate. Any marriage that contains these elements can do nothing *but* succeed.[1]

Whenever I find myself at odds with my husband (or anyone else) I pull out I Corinthians 13 and give myself a check-up or do an inventory of my love walk. I especially like the Amplified Version because it leaves no doubt as to what it is saying. One hundred percent of the time, I find that I am deficient in one area or another. I find that I am either inflated with pride, insisting on my own rights, or taking account of the wrong that was done to me. At that point, I usually go back to my husband and ask for his forgiveness for my having made the choice to do things my own way instead of God's.

Even the very best of relationships have room for growth. Let's make the habit of only comparing ourselves to God's Word to see how we pass muster. He will always show us areas where we can improve, and that is because He loves us and wants us to become more and more like His Son. When we find ourselves lacking, we can cry out to Him; and He will gently lift us up, encourage us and get us back on track.

DAY FIFTY-SIX
Prophesy to the Four Winds!
(Pam)

Ezekiel 37:4-5 *(NLT) Then he said to me, "Speak to these bones and say, 'Dry bones, listen to the word of the LORD! This is what the Sovereign LORD says: Look! I am going to breathe into you and make you live again!*

Most of us know the story of when God took Ezekiel, in a vision, to what is commonly known as the Valley of Dry Bones. These bones were once people, the people of Israel slain in battle. They had been dead so long, they were now skeletons, and their skeletons had been in this valley so long that the bones were now bleached and dry. There was absolutely no sign of life in them. However, as Ezekiel looked over this valley, God told him to speak or prophesy to those bones and command them to hear the word of the Lord that told them that they will live again. God later told Ezekiel to prophesy to the four winds that they would bring breath into these bodies.

There are so many marriages out there – yours may be one of them – that look like there is no possible life left in them. The damage has been so devastating that it appears there is no possible hope for it. The love that once filled their hearts has now been replaced with hatred and bitterness.

I know in my heart that God wants to miraculously restore those broken marriages. I prophesy to those dead, dry marriages and say, "Hear the word of the Lord: 'Rise up and live, again! Take your broken heart and place it in My Loving Hands and watch as I massage it back to life and make it whole.'"

Now, I want to challenge you to prophesy to your own marriage! Take the hand of your spouse or someone with whom you can agree and begin to prophesy to the four winds and command them to bring the breath and life of God back into your marriage. This is a bold step; but if you can grasp hold of the whole measure of faith God had given you, I believe, with all my heart, that God will show up in a spectacular way and blow your mind! Let your faith soar to the highest heights possible and see God do the impossible. Jeremiah 32:27 reminds us, "I am the LORD, the God of all the peoples of the world. Is anything too hard for me?" (NLT). A rhetorical question, but the answer is a resounding, NO! You have already discovered that *your* way does not work; now try it God's way.

God wants your marriage to live again. He isn't willing to give up on you; don't give up on Him, and don't give up on each other! Give it one more try! Take the limits off God and allow Him to manifest Himself in your marriage in a phenomenal way!

DAY FIFTY-SEVEN
The Grass is Greenest Where It's Watered
(Pam)

"The Grass is always greener on the other side." Everyone is so familiar with that quote, and most of us have wised up enough to realize that it's hardly ever true.

I remember when Adrian and I bought our first home. As we first arrived, we saw how manicured our new lawn and other landscaping were; we beamed with pride. It was the cutest house ever, and we were so excited until we understood how much upkeep was required to keep it looking that cute. It did, eventually, show need of better care.

We didn't know anything about how to care for a lawn but were determined to learn. We would sometimes look with envy at our neighbors' yards and wish we could do better. One day, while doing some yard work, we walked over to our neighbor's just to say hi since he was out. We were rather surprised, once we actually got in the yard, to see all the multi-colored grass. In other words, some of it was brown, some light green and some dark green. For some reason, you just couldn't tell that from the perspective of our front door.

We did notice another neighbor who seemed to

water his lawn incessantly. He was out there fertilizing and tending to it as if it were the most precious thing in the world. When we got close enough to really see it, we expected to see the same multi-colored grass as our other neighbor. To our delight, his lawn really was green and lush, just as it appeared from far away. We learned a lot from him that day.

Do other people's marriages look better to you than yours does? When you get close, do you see the spots that look neglected or diseased? Perhaps you know someone whose marriage really is as vibrant and healthy as it looks. If so, it's because they are watering it incessantly. They are not allowing neglect and carelessness to take over. They are working on it as if it is the most precious thing in the world.

Let me encourage you to tend to the garden of your marriage. Make it a priority. Be willing to fertilize and nurture it with the Word of God it until it becomes what you want it to be – not just in appearance, but in reality.

Ephesians 5:33 *Nevertheless let each one of you in particular so love his own wife as himself, and let the wife see that she respects her husband.*

DAY FIFTY-EIGHT
Pray
(Adrian)

Luke 18:1 *(AMPC) Also [Jesus] told them a parable to the effect that they ought always to pray and not to turn coward (faint, lose heart, and give up).*

We live in an age where it appears that we struggle for every precious moment of personal time. The many inventions that were supposed to save us time have deceptively stolen time and attention from so many coveted activities and relationships. I know that electronic gadgets have changed the dynamics of my home interactions so that it requires a concerted, deliberate effort to communicate face to face.

In today's Scripture, Jesus was encouraging His disciples to make a consistent practice to communicate with God. Jesus told them they ought always to pray and not faint. Various translations of the word for faint have been used and are listed above, but the bottom line is that we cannot give up on prayer. Our success as Christ's followers depends on our continued communication with God through prayer. God desires relationship with us and has designed prayer as the vehicle of expression and understanding. Make prayer a habit that will please God forever.

In our marriages, communication is a critical component to a sound and healthy marriage. You know that things can unravel very quickly if you do not talk and spend personal, intimate time with your spouse. No matter how bad you may think things have become, they will only get worse without loving, patient communication with God and each other.

The parable that Jesus told His disciples in the verse above had to do with being persistent. Many times, we think that because we have said something once that should settle it, but God and our mates appreciate determined persistence. I don't believe that God is resistant to our prayers but likes us to demonstrate our faith, patience, hope, and yes, love through our continued, dogged determination to ask – believing that He cares. I'm not talking about annoying repetition of requests but an ever-present thankful expression of our faith that He hears and will do what He has promised.

As with God, we need to continually communicate the love and dedication we have for our spouses. It may appear that our deeds and words are being ignored; but never give up. Don't turn coward and confess that better communications will not help, or lose heart by believing there is no hope. We ought to always pray to God believing that all things are possible for those who trust Him. Continue to seek opportunities to communicate with your spouse, and fight for the time, believing it pays great rewards in strengthening our relationships. Make time to pray for your spouse.

DAY FIFTY-NINE
Devoted Familiarity
(Adrian)

Psalm 78:35-37 *(NLT) Then they remembered that God was their rock, that God Most High was their redeemer. But all they gave him was lip service; they lied to him with their tongues. Their hearts were not loyal to him. They did not keep his covenant.*

Psalms 78 provides a summary of the relationship and interactions recorded in the Bible between God and the Israelites. From the very beginning, God has desired a personal and intimate relationship with mankind starting in the Garden of Eden. It was there that God expressed His love for man by creating the institution we call marriage, authorizing and blessing the male-female union.

The verses above describe how the Israelites acknowledged God with their mouths but not with their hearts. Yes, they remembered how God had gotten them out of some tight situations, but this did not result in devotion or loyalty. Scripture says that they gave God lip service and lied to Him, and maybe, themselves. The defining statement for the condition of the Israelites was that their hearts were not loyal to God – loyal being defined as characterized by showing faithfulness to commitments, vows, allegiances, obligations, etc. In other words, they did not keep their covenant or reverence. They had become familiar with God and his covenant but had failed to experience true devotion to their Covenant God.

Familiarity can be a great intimacy-building experience that can also become dangerous to any relationship when callousness is allowed to breed. God desires us to know His character, will, and commitment to us as defined in His word. It is through the awe and expressed love in God's Word, along with our personal life experience with God, that opens our eyes, heart, and mind to His ever-present love for us. This recognition allows us to enjoy the comfort, peace, security, and hope promised by God to those who love and know Him. When we allow our familiarity to cause us to take Him for granted and not appreciate the loving sacrifice and provision made through Christ Jesus daily, it can become dangerous to a healthy relationship. In the same way, our relationship with our spouse that started out full of wonder, excitement, intrigue, and love can become callously unhealthy without continued acts and attitudes of respect.

Protecting our relationships with God and our mate requires us to always value, honor, and respect them. We must remember the life experiences that have been shared and crafted together over time. Remember and be grateful for the love received and the opportunity afforded to love and develop eternal and life-long bonds. Familiarity that intentionally breeds devotion through mutual appreciation is God's plan, purpose, and will for humanity.

Devotion to God and your spouse will allow the benefits of God's promises to manifest in your life. Our challenge is to be truly loyal and committed to developing an ever- stronger and intimate relationship by valuing, honoring, and appreciating our loved ones. The trap is to mistake familiarity for devotion. The Israelites knew what God wanted and would conform periodically, just as we do in our marriages. The acts of love must someday be transformed into relational heart-anchored, love-spawned acts and deeds of affectionate commitments that are stronger than our love of life itself. Keeping our covenant with God first and then our spouse must become the true meaning of life itself to us.

DAY SIXTY
If My Marriage Were a Reality Show...
(Pam)

2 Corinthians 3:2 *(MSG) You yourselves are all the endorsement we need. Your very lives are a letter that anyone can read by just looking at you.*

Haven't you ever looked at people and wondered what their lives were really like at home? Anyone can put on a pretty good charade out in public, but what happens when they get behind those closed doors?

Suppose you were approached by a television producer and asked if you would be willing to put your marriage on display in a reality show? Of course, they will pay you handsomely for each season. Here's the kicker, though: They want to use your show as a teaching tool for pre-marrieds. Would you be delighted or terrified at the idea? The next question is: Will your show be used as a training manual for what *to do* or what *not to do*?

The truth is that we don't have to have a reality show that is broadcasted nationwide to be an example to others. People are watching us all the time – learning from us, emulating us or even retreating from our behavior in pursuit of something better.

We've heard it over and over, "You are the only Bible someone will ever read." With that in mind, we ought to want to be the best examples possible; not so we can brag or pat ourselves on the back, but to be able to help someone and make their journey a little easier. I am a firm believer in learning from other people's experiences – what to avoid and what to embrace.

Married life is one of the greatest blessings as well as one of the toughest battles you will experience in life. I am determined to leave an example of faith, courage, and obedience to God's Word for others to follow. If *my* marriage were a reality show, it would have some comedy, some tears, some drama, some failures, great joys, and great victories.

If your marriage were a reality show, it would have _____. How would you fill in the blank? Who's watching you? Don't disappoint them. Allow God to help you be a testimony of His greatness. Allow others to see where God took something broken and put it back together so much better than new; or where He took something that was good and made it extraordinary!

Smile wide, the camera's rolling!

DAY SIXTY-ONE
Too Much Information
(Pam)

Ephesians 4:15 *(MSG) God wants us to grow up, to know the whole truth and tell it in love - like Christ in everything. We take our lead from Christ, who is the source of everything we do.*

Do you always like hearing the truth? If we are honest, most of us must admit that there are times when we would rather not hear the truth in certain situations. We don't always want to know that we look fat, or that the particular outfit we are wearing is unflattering, or that the meal we spent hours preparing is tasteless.

I am discovering that telling the truth in our society is something people use only if it works for a particular situation. In other words, if it is a benefit to tell the truth they will do it, otherwise…. Why do we do that? Many times, it is either to keep ourselves out of trouble or to prevent hurting someone's feelings.

We regard the truth as sacred in our home. Our children were taught, growing up, that a person who lies cannot be trusted. One day my daughters asked me a question. "Since I don't want to lie, what can I say to a friend who asks if I like her outfit when I don't?" My response was, "Simply tell her, 'Wow, that's so interesting!" Now, of course, whenever any of us uses that term to describe anything, we will look at each other a bit suspiciously. It's kind of a private joke with us.

One of the issues I still deal with is hearing the truth from my husband when something is bothering him. When I can tell he is out of sorts, I will quiz him as to what is bothering him. He will just blow it off until I practically badger him to death. Then, of course, he will tell me the truth, the whole truth, and nothing but the truth. Sometimes it hurts, but I asked for it. If I didn't want the truth, I should have left him alone. Sometimes, we just ask for too much information, and we get it right between the eyes! One thing I can attest to is that he is never mean or harsh when delivering that truth, but sometimes, the truth just plain hurts.

The Scripture above tells us that God wants us to know the truth, and He wants us to tell the truth in love. There is a dying world out there that needs to know the truth about Jesus, but we cannot afford to bash people's heads in with that truth. We must deliver the message of the Gospel with love because "God is love" (1 John 4:8 KJV). His Word also tells us, "… therefore with lovingkindness have I drawn thee (Jer. 31:3b KJV).

In our marriages, we need to remember that if we don't want to hear the truth from our spouse, we'd better not ask the question; but if the truth is precious, we will hear it and receive it as something that will help us. When we share the truth with our mate, let's remember to share it in love. Just because something is true, we don't have to inflict harm to make that truth known. I challenge you to hear the truth and speak the truth, and always do both in love.

DAY SIXTY-TWO

Do You Talk Too Much?
(Pam)

Proverbs 17:27a, 28 *(NIV) The one who has knowledge uses words with restraint…, Even fools are thought wise if they keep silent, and discerning if they hold their tongues.*

Proverbs 18:2,13 *Fools have no interest in understanding; they only want to air their own opinions. Spouting off before listening to the facts is both shameful and foolish.*

Proverbs 10:19 *(NLT) Too much talk leads to sin. Be sensible and keep your mouth shut.*

A great deal of the conflicts that occur in marital relationships is due to just plain talking too much. You might be asking the question, "How can issues be resolved if we don't talk?" What I'm talking about are the things that cause conflicts in the first place. How can you tell if you talk too much? I'm glad you asked.

Some years ago, the comedian, Jeff Foxworthy, had a routine that went something like this: "If you_____ _____, you're probably a redneck". With that same format, I will throw out some scenarios for you to consider:

- If you find it necessary to make a critical comment on your spouse's clothing selection, you probably talk too much. In most cases, if your spouse chose that particular outfit, it's what he wanted to wear. Remember, he's a grown-up and capable of making his own decisions.

- If, when your mate comes to you with a problem she needs help solving, you find yourself developing a solution before all the facts are presented, you probably talk too much. In order to give good advice, it's critically important to be a good listener. If you are already formulating your solution, you have stopped listening. You don't hear your partner anymore; you only hear your own thoughts. (See Pro. 18:13)

- If you find it necessary to correct your partner every time he relays a story to someone with a few of the details misspoken, you probably talk too much. What is your motive in the correction? Is it to embarrass your mate and make yourself look good? What harm is there, really, if some of the details are wrong?

- If you find it necessary to correct every mispronounced word your spouse speaks, you probably talk too much. If you're not careful, you will come off with an air of superiority that's offensive and certainly does not promote marital harmony. Your spouse is not your child who needs constant correction.

- If you find that you just can't let go of an issue until you have been fully heard, you probably talk too much. Sometimes we can talk and talk and push and push, thinking that our talking and pushing will bring resolution when all it does is cause alienation. There are times when, even if we feel misunderstood, we ought to let stuff go. If it's a serious issue, then, by all means, work it out. But if it's not a life altering thing, don't try to talk it to death. Let it go!

These are just a very few examples where we, perhaps,

speak a little more than we should. I'm sure you can come up with many of your own scenarios. When we talk too much, we create more problems than we solve; we hurt more than we help. When we do speak, let's let our words be words of comfort, words of encouragement, words of affirmation.

DAY SIXTY-THREE
The Umpire
(Adrian)

Colossians 3:15 *(NLT) And let the peace that comes from Christ rule in your hearts. For as members of one body you are called to live in peace. And always be thankful.*

True peace in life is the peace that is a gift from God that is established and accompanies His grace provided through Christ. This peace is a personal blessing meant to also establish peace in the body or fellowship of Christ. The word rule used in the above Scripture means to umpire, as its original meaning came from an athletic setting. So, what is being said here is that peace is to be the umpire in our lives when it comes to making decisions regarding issues of disputes and establishing priorities or direction. In the same manner that an umpire, during a sporting event, settles questions regarding proper play, peace should the deciding factor in our personal and interpersonal affairs as Christians.

The meaning of the word peace speaks of being bound together; that is, to be unified into integrated oneness. The context of this Scripture was speaking to the unity of the body of Christ, but I believe God is also very interested in the unity of our marriages and families. Christian relationships are not just directed person-to-person but should always be conducted in consideration of our personal relationship with Christ. Because of our appreciation of the peace experienced with God and our desire to share and maintain this wonderful gift, our challenge and goal is to seek God's will and purpose for all our relationships.

By being mindful of the grace and peace provided by God through Jesus Christ, we will let peace guide and umpire our actions. God desires us to be united in oneness, and we need to ask, "Will our attitudes, decisions and resulting actions bring us closer to Him and each other?" Setting God's peace as our priority will change our personal lives and help to shape the environment in our homes and wherever we go.

Let peace be the umpire - the deciding factor - in how you pursue life's relationships. This will not always allow you to avoid conflict, but make peace your objective. Be thankful for the gift of peace you have received from God, and let it inspire you to be a peacemaker.

DAY SIXTY-FOUR
Fundamentals
(Adrian)

Revelation 2:5 *Remember therefore from where you have fallen; repent and do the first works, or else I will come to you quickly and remove your lampstand from its place—unless you repent.*

I looked up the meaning of fundamental and found it to be defined as: pertaining to or constituting a foundation; basic; primary; essential. In the verse above, the Apostle John quotes a message from Jesus to the church of Ephesus, designed to inspire a sense of urgency for renewed commitment to their relationship with Christ. When I thought of the fundamentals of the marriage relationship, I was reminded of this Scripture.

Sometimes in our relationship with Christ and our spouses, we tend to let slip the basic and primary foundations of our connection. The words of appreciation, adoration, and just acts and expressions of love that seemed to flow so easily from our lips and hands have dried up or become lost in the passage of time and familiarity. The places you use to frequent and the activities so often shared have been replaced with lifeless or thoughtless habits that only provide a shadow of the intensity once demonstrated between you and your mate.

I would like to encourage you regarding your marriage, as Christ did the church of Ephesus, to repent of your lack of passion and once again practice the basic, yet essential, show of attention that won the heart and commitment of your spouse. Remember the excitement that the very sight and sound of your mate use to bring to you. Resurrect some of the activities and confessions of the past but infuse them with the excitement and knowledge gained through the experience afforded by time spent together.

You may not have the strength or physical stamina of the past, but the thoughts, and true meanings and values of the shared memories can inspire you to devote more time to express your sincere feelings today. Determine to never let the excitement and soul commitment for your relationship diminish. Strive to find ways to not only maintain the fundamentals of your relationship but to build upon their foundational bonds that will draw you closer and even more in love with your spouse than at the start.

Do your first works and see if your skills at perpetuating a love that grows sweeter everyday can be developed and sustained.

DAY SIXTY-FIVE
Warts and All
(Pam)

Ephesians 1:4-5 *(NLT) Long ago, even before he made the world, God loved us and chose us in Christ to be holy and without fault in his eyes. His unchanging plan has always been to adopt us into his own family by bringing us to himself through Jesus Christ. And this gave him great pleasure.*

Doesn't it just astound you how God can make the decision to love us despite all of our many faults and shortcomings, especially when we understand how much He abhors sin? It's only because of the redemptive work that was done on the cross through Jesus' death, burial and resurrection that we could find such favor with God. We could not have earned or received it any other way.

How easy it is for us to forget how flawed we are when it comes to loving and accepting other people. We somehow believe that, before we can fully love our mates, they have to be perfect. God did not make His decision to love us based on how undefective we were; He loved us as though we already were. God wants us to give each other that same gift.

If you have ever watched the movie Shrek, you will recall how Fiona fell in love with Shrek despite the fact that he was an ogre, literally, and even though she was a beautiful princess, at the time. It was discovered that Fiona had a curse placed on her that would turn *her* into an ogre at night. When she realized that she loved Shrek, warts and all, she actually transformed into an ogre, herself, permanently. The profundity of that movie is that Fiona did not reject Shrek because he was not perfect; she did not place herself in a superior position and look down on him. She understood that she, too, was sometimes an ogre. She was able to look past all the imperfections and still love him because she knew *she* was not perfect.

God wants us to love each other, warts and all. When we recognize what God has done for us, we should want to share that gift with our spouse. May God help us to remember that we are all wretches undone, without Jesus, and may we help each other to enjoy the benefits and joy of unconditional love – love that says, "You don't have to be flawless for me to pour all my love on you, without reservation. I choose to love you fully, and look past the flaws and into your heart to see you through God's eyes."

DAY SIXTY-SIX
Letting Go of Bitterness
(Pam)

When people get married, they plan to have a loving relationship. Their expectations are very high. Suddenly, an offense takes place. It's not dealt with; then more offenses come that are not dealt with and soon bitterness and resentment set in. You may not even notice it at first. It starts so quietly, but then it begins destroying your relationship.

When you find yourself being easily irritated with or very critical towards your spouse, you should realize that some bitterness has begun to set in. Bitterness is a result of pride and selfishness, and these are two of the major killers in a marriage. God wants to bring healing to our marriages, and He wants us to eliminate all resentment. Eph. 4:31 tells us to, "Let all bitterness…be put away from you …"

The reason that bitterness is so harmful is that it gives us justification for being mean, cold, short-tempered or unpleasant to others. You won't feel guilty if you are able to justify your behavior. Feeling guilty is what causes our conscience to kick in and prevent us from doing things we know are wrong. One author put it this way: "Our conscience tells us that it is wrong to do evil to others. This limits the expression of our hatred towards others. If people are going to persist in their meanness toward someone, they need some way to override the guilt function of their conscience. Otherwise guilt would pile on so thick that they would have to stop being mean. They feel bad (guilty) about it. Bitterness provides the needed short circuit that allows them to bypass the work of their conscience, not only to do evil to others but even to feel smug and self-righteous about it."[1]

Bitterness can defile our relationship. Hebrews 12:15 states, "looking carefully lest anyone fall short of the grace of God; lest any root of bitterness springing up cause trouble, and by this many become defiled." This Scripture makes it clear that a bitter root that springs up causes trouble. It not only affects the bitter person, but spreads into the lives of others. Bitterness happens because we are expecting our mates to be perfect even though *we* are not.

Let us pray that we are always able to give grace to our mates and learn to deal with issues quickly and lovingly so that no root of bitterness springs up in our lives or marriage.

DAY SIXTY-SEVEN
New Every Morning
(Adrian)

Lamentations 3:21-23 *(NLT) Yet I still dare to hope when I remember this: The faithful love of the Lord never ends! His mercies never cease. Great is his faithfulness; his mercies begin afresh each morning.*

Many of us have been or are in a position of lamenting the events of the past that have brought us to the pain and anguish of today. We have done things in our lives and marriage relationships that we regret and truly seek forgiveness from and restoration with God, love ones, and friends. Jeremiah was grieving over the sins and degradation of Judah that resulted in them going into captivity, but in the middle of all his sadness he writes the Scriptures quoted above. Jeremiah found hope in the faithfulness of God's desire and character to provide an opportunity for restoration to fallen mankind - us in particular.

I believe that God has demonstrated His love and forgiveness toward us so that we can share these gifts with others, especially our spouse and family. The same kindness and unconditional love experienced from God through the life, death, and resurrection of Jesus Christ must be imitated and distributed. Think about the hope that we have today because we dared to believe and embrace the love call of God. Remember the despair that was obliterated by the grace and mercy dispensed by God and His plan of redemption. Imagine if you can, convincing your spouse that *your* mercies and love are renewed every morning along with God's.

One must truly understand that the God who knows everything there is to know about you has promised to supply His mercy to your life every morning without fail based on your believing in His faithfulness to you. How inspiring it is to appreciate the freedom and joy of knowing that the mistakes, failures, and sins of yesterday are forgiven and a new provision of mercy has been allocated for each day of your life. Let's allow our gratitude toward God to stimulate us to solicit Him to help us display mercy, forgiveness, and love for our spouses. No one on earth knows our shortcomings, failures, character flaws, victories, strengths, weaknesses, and ambitions better than our mates. What more awe-inspiring gift to give each other each day than a fresh supply of mercy and love.

You can only give it if you have first received it from God for yourself. God is the only one with an endless stream of mercy and love. When we tap into His resources, He will allow us to be His distributor and representative to our mates first and then the world.

DAY SIXTY-EIGHT
Be a Light Bearer
(Adrian)

Matthew 5:14-16 *(NLT) "You are the light of the world—like a city on a hilltop that cannot be hidden. No one lights a lamp and then puts it under a basket. Instead, a lamp is placed on a stand, where it gives light to everyone in the house. In the same way, let your good deeds shine out for all to see, so that everyone will praise your heavenly Father.*

The Scriptures quoted above are part of Jesus' Sermon on the Mount. In this sermon, Jesus described his followers as the "light of the world". Christ came to be the Light of the world and has empowered those who believe in Him, and are willing to follow His example, to transmit His light through their lives. Jesus has not given us this light to be hidden from the world but has instructed us that its proper place is to be a place of prominence, on a light stand. The purpose of the light was to give guidance to everyone in the house and world, pointing to and prompting praise of our God.

I want to challenge you as God's light bearer to let your God-inspired deeds shine first in your home and marriage and amongst your children and other family members. Your family and spouse need to see, hear, and experience the inspiring effect that Christ has upon every area of your life. They need to experience the love, acceptance, and forgiveness that you have received from Christ, flowing from you towards them, unobstructed by the shadow of hidden sins. The light that is in you can dispel the darkness and begin to expose the lies of a world that tries to deny the benefits reaped from embracing the life, love, and light of Christ.

Our homes are to be the practice and proving grounds of the influence of Christ on our personal lives. Our spouse and children should be able to attest to the blessing of having Christ illuminate their home. Let them see you studying God's Word, praying, being thankful, and full of joy and love. From your example of a love for God's Word and His people, patience, forgiveness, and pursuit of peace with others, our spouses and families will also be encouraged to receive Christ's light in their lives. Don't be afraid to be an example of a Christ-filled life, and commit to boldly explain why you are willing to yield your life to Christ.

Ephesians 5:8 *(NLT) For once you were full of darkness, but now you have light from the Lord. So live as people of light!*

Be a light bearer and bring life and light to your home and the world around you.

DAY SIXTY-NINE
Embrace His Presence, Part 2
(Adrian)

Psalm 139:1-4 *(NLT) O Lord, you have examined my heart and know everything about me. You know when I sit down or stand up. You know my thoughts even when I'm far away. You see me when I travel and when I rest at home. You know everything I do. You know what I am going to say even before I say it, Lord.*

In Hebrews 13:5-6, God promises to never leave or forsake us. What many of us fail to understand is that the presence of God is an expression of His love for us. This verse goes on to say that the reason for His faithfulness is that he desires for us to be able to boldly declare, "God is my helper". Until we can truly comprehend the depth of God's love for us as an individual, it is difficult to joyfully accept the longing God has for involvement in our lives.

We have coached many people over the years and found some to believe that their marriage, home, and family were areas of their personal domain. The thought was that these are areas free from the intervention of God or that they were on their own in a trial adventure. Many of us are willing to allow God access when trouble ensues, illness is attacking, or rescue is needed but still demand the control back once delivered. It needs to be understood that God's promised love takes the form of being ever-present, involved, caringly attentive, and eternally desirous of a loving relationship with us.

God's presence reaches, covers, manifest, and dominates anywhere and everywhere we are or are not. The only condition for full enjoyment of this love gift is for us to accept and embrace God, the Giver. Acknowledge and ask God through Christ to be involved in every aspect of your life. Exclude Him from no activity, thought, or area of your existence. Invite Him to be the true Lord of your life and then expand His lordship to your marriage, home, and family. Understand that because of God's love for you, you want Him involved and influencing every aspect of you and your marriage.

Realize that God knows everything there is to know about you and He still loves and desires to have relationship with you. Even if you thought you could, or still wanted to hide from God, it's impossible. Grasp hold of God's loving presence and allow Him to work in you, on you, and through you to become personally blessed and to be a blessing to your family. Realize that there is nothing in this life that God has assigned you to handle without Him. As promised, God is always present; but when we focus our attention on Him, we become conscious of His preexisting, loving attendance.

In order to please God, we must believe that He is, and that he desires to reward us for our faith in Him.

DAY SEVENTY
Are You Saying Enough?
(Pam)

Proverbs 3:27 *(NIV) Do not withhold good from those to whom it is due, when it is in your power to act.*

Proverbs 16:24 *(NLT) Kind words are like honey— sweet to the soul and healthy for the body.*

In an earlier devotional, I challenged you to determine if you talk too much. In other words, are you constantly critical or belittling or just being a poor listener? Today, I want to test you in a different area: How well are you using the words you should be speaking?

Sometimes, it is very easy to overlook the good things our mates do for us. We can take them for granted and never acknowledge the care and concern they exhibit towards us. We see it but never take the time to express our appreciation for it. How many times have you requested that your spouse do something a certain way or not do something a certain way? They fulfill your request only to have you completely ignore it or fail to acknowledge it.

Everyone wants to be affirmed and appreciated even if they never articulate it. In referencing the two Scriptures above, we see that we are first admonished not to withhold good from someone when we are fully able to be a blessing. We can bless with our words. Next we are told that kind words are like honey. It's both deliciously sweet and healthy. After reading that verse, I wanted to find out what the health benefits of honey truly are. I was quite impressed to discover that it can improve digestion, lessen muscle fatigue, boost energy, and suppress coughs. There are several more, but the most surprising was that it is touted to help heal cuts. Apparently, when you apply honey directly to a minor wound, in addition to preventing infection, it also works to reduce pain, lessen pus and odor, and helps to promote a faster recovery so that your cut heals quickly and has a lesser chance of scarring.

    I want you to catch a glimpse of the potency of your generous and thoughtful words. Just imagine how healing and helpful our words can be. We need to encourage one another. When we feel heartened and uplifted, our whole outlook on life changes. That's a gift we can give to our mates. We can inspire them to greatness just by paying attention to them and acknowledging their contribution to our life and the lives of others. Everyone needs an "atta boy" now and then. It means the most when it comes from the person who loves us the most. Are you saying enough?

DAY SEVENTY-ONE
Bragging on Your Husband
(Pam)

Ephesians 4:29 *(NLT) ...Let everything you say be good and helpful, so that your words will be an encouragement to those who hear them.*

A friend's dear husband died a few years ago. While he was hospitalized, and it was clear that the end was near, we went to spend time with her and her beloved. While he slept peacefully, we chatted quietly with our friend and also listened intently as she reviewed all the wonderful qualities of her husband.

Although we knew her husband pretty well, it was so revealing to hear stories from the perspective of someone who lived with him on a daily basis. She told us of the different musical bands he had been involved in and bragged about his musical arrangement abilities and the fact that he could play just about any instrument you put in his hands. She spoke of his tenderness and kindness and other things like that.

Despite the difficulty of the situation in which she found herself, our friend's face just lit up when she shared memories of her husband. They had been married for over 20 years, and they had a great marriage. I'm certain it had not been perfect – no marriage is –

but not once did she mention any of his bad habits, or mistakes, or bad decisions. She only concentrated on the good.

Why must we wait until a time of crisis such as this one to remember the wonderful qualities of our spouses? Why do we so easily major on the negatives instead of the positives? I heard a story of when one woman was questioned as to why she didn't divorce her husband over an infidelity. She answered, "I decided to be thankful for nine things he did right instead damning him for the one thing he did wrong." What a powerful statement! How many of us could take that attitude? But it's true. We get so caught up in the one or two things our husbands don't do correctly and totally forget about all the good they do.

It's time we start bragging on our mates! Let's begin to tell the world how wonderful they are; and by all means, let's not only tell the world, let's tell our beloved mates, too. In fact, let's tell them, first. Periodically, my husband and I each create a list of each other's good qualities, and then we exchange them for the other to read. Our goal is to outdo the other in how long our list is. Sometimes, they do get quite lengthy.

I'm convinced that if we concentrate on the positives, the negatives will eventually fade into oblivion. Perhaps that is my optimistic nature talking, but it's what I truly believe. As women, we have a tendency to complain a lot, and we need to really check ourselves in that area. At times, we have so many rules we don't give our husbands any breathing room. I'm not really sure why we expect them to be perfect when we aren't.

I want to offer you a challenge. For the next full week, try exchanging any complaint you are tempted to convey for a bragging session aimed at your husband. I'm certain you will be amazed by what God will reveal to you about him. Be prepared to pick him up off the floor, afterwards, as he is sure to be shocked.

DAY SEVENTY-TWO
Fascinating!
(Pam)

Song of Solomon 4:9 *(NLT) You have captured my heart, my treasure, my bride. You hold it hostage with one glance of your eyes, with a single jewel of your necklace.*

Do you remember when you first started dating your spouse? It was a very special time of getting to know one another and observing different characteristics – things that made each of you interesting or even fascinating.

You probably observed the way the other held utensils while eating, or even how he used his napkins. You were very careful to notice what he was wearing and how clean or messy he was. I'm sure you watched her walk across a room, observing the sway of her hips. And, of course, you listened to the sound of her voice with all its varied inflections and tones.

This is what we do when we are making a decision as to how far a relationship will go. We pay attention to EVERYTHING! Something happens, however, once we've committed ourselves to someone. Over a period of time, if we are not careful, we become very nonchalant about our connection. We begin to feel like we know everything there is to know about our mate, and so we start taking him for granted. This casualness then causes us to focus our attentions elsewhere, other than the needs and desires of our companion.

It's easy to fall into the trap of complacency, so we have to be intentional about continuing our pursuit of our spouse. My husband has said on numerous occasions that he learns something new about me at least once a week. He enjoys sitting at the kitchen counter while I am preparing dinner because he likes to keep one eye on the TV and one eye on me. I caught him watching me one day and challenged him, "Why are you staring at me?" He responded, "I find you fascinating." He went on to explain that he likes how I move or the expressions on my face when I'm trying to figure out a particular recipe. He even likes how I might gaze off into space looking very contemplative. Why I fascinate my husband, I have no clue; but I'm so glad that I do. I don't look forward to the time when I become boring to him.

Ask God to help you get back on track to treasuring your prize. Begin anew, having a goal to find something new and fascinating about your beloved. Trust me, you don't know everything there is to know. Get ready for some surprises and delights. This does require you, of course, to look for positive things while ignoring the negative ones. Accentuate the positive, eliminate the negative, latch on to the affirmative, and don't mess with Mr. In-between. Do you remember that old Bing Crosby song?

DAY SEVENTY-THREE
Seeking God's Face Together
(Pam)

Do you and your spouse pray together? I have posed that question to many of the couples Adrian and I coach who are having serious troubles in their marriage. The unfortunate answer from nearly all of them is, "No."

I say it's unfortunate because I know in my heart that part of the difficulty they are having is because they have not understood, nor tapped into, the power they can use to keep the enemy from shattering their lives: Praying in agreement together.

Praying together can be one of the most intimate times a couple can spend with each other. As you petition God, you are able to hear each other's heart and be touched by the words that pour out. I can imagine that may seem a bit threatening if it has not already become a habit. However, if you are able to get passed that fear, you will discover a depth to your relationship you didn't know could exist.

Let's look at the Word: "Again I say to you that if **two** of you **agree** on earth concerning anything that they ask, it will be done for them by My Father in heaven." Matthew 18:19.

A couple praying together is a major threat to Satan's kingdom which is why he works overtime to make sure it doesn't happen. God's Word tells us that when two persons agree concerning anything they are asking God for, they can expect to receive it simply because they believe it and agree on it.

Make it your goal to find time to pray together. It won't solve all your problems, but it will surely get you on the right path as you seek God together for solutions.

DAY SEVENTY-FOUR
Happily, Ever After
(Pam)

Ephesians 5:22-23 *(The Message) Wives, understand and support your husbands in ways that show your support for Christ.*

The husband provides leadership to his wife the way Christ does to his church, not by domineering but by cherishing

These Scriptures represent the ideal husband and wife relationship. Seems simple enough, yet, in so many cases, appears so unattainable.

Remember all the fairy tales you read as a child? They always started with: "Once upon a time…" and ended with: "And they lived happily ever after". When you get past the opening statement, there are a lot of other things that go on in the story. You have the setting, the characters, the plot, the conflict, the climax and the resolution.

Now just imagine your married life as one of those fairy tales. What would it read like? The setting is your marriage; you and your mate are the characters. Within a story, the two main characters represent a protagonist and an antagonist – a good guy and a bad guy. Which one are you? As is normal in most marriages, each of you will play either role at one time or another until you are both fully conformed into the image of Christ.

The plot of your marriage is how you live your everyday life until you experience a conflict. That soon reaches a climax. How will it be resolved? Amicably?

My point is this: there is a lot of life to live before you can get to the "happily ever after". There will always be conflict, climax and resolution in your relationship, but that should not deter you from pursuing your happy ending. Once you have made up your mind that your marriage is a forever one, those conflicts become fewer and fewer.

What would it take to create your "happily ever after"? For one thing, it should be a determination to never give up on your mate or yourself. Contrary to popular belief, a happy marriage is not just a fairy tale when we allow God to have the preeminence in our lives. It is reality if we trust the Holy Spirit to guide and assist us in our marital journey.

DAY SEVENTY-FIVE
Who's Got Your Back?
(Adrian)

Psalm 139:5-6

5 You have hedged me behind and before, And laid Your hand upon me.

6 Such knowledge is too wonderful for me; It is high, I cannot attain it.

In the Scriptures above, the Psalmist was expressing his belief that God had hedged him in. The hedge indicates being surrounded, protected, or limited. Some might even say that he was boxed in. The Psalmist was making this declaration with excitement knowing that the God of the universe was concerned enough about him that He had surrounded and was committed to protect him. He goes on to say that the Lord had laid His hand on him allowing for a personal relationship to be developed. This whole concept and reality of God having his back was knowledge too wonderful to fully grasp or comprehend.

I think many today have the same feelings or inability to fully comprehend the level and extent of God's love and protection for His people. I believe that when we are able to experience the depth of God's commitment to us, then we are empowered to share and exercise confidence and security with others. When we understand what God has done for us through His love, we want to share it. I want to encourage you to share this knowledge and exhilaration with your spouse and family each day.

We sometimes are quick to say to one another that we have each other's back, but can they really feel our hand on their back providing support. The Psalmist had been through some experiences that made him know that God was present and He cared. In our marriages, we must make every effort to convey our love and support for each other. This becomes an assignment and opportunity to express the sense and reality of being committed to the success of our spouse - defining success as only being achieved when both of you are pleased and satisfied that your mate is surrounded by your love. There is no greater feeling of love, security and contentment than knowing God's has your back, but the second best is being secure and assured enough to help your mate experience the commitment of knowing you also have their back, come what may.

Make a commitment to study and get to know God well enough that you have the assurance of Him having your back, and then commit to the daily expression and exercise of that love received from God to your mate and family.

DAY SEVENTY-SIX
Live Considerately
(Adrian)

1 Peter 3:7 *Amplified Bible (AMPC) In the same way you married men should live considerately with [your wives], with an intelligent recognition [of the marriage relation], honoring the woman as [physically] the weaker, but [realizing that you] are joint heirs of the grace (God's unmerited favor) of life, in order that your prayers may not be hindered and cut off. [Otherwise you cannot pray effectively.]*

In many situations or practices of life, we like to look to examples of people around us to emulate. Seeing a living example can make the activity we desire to perform more obtainable and executable. As husbands trying to be men of God regarding our everyday conduct toward our spouses and family, it may be hard to find godly examples of loving husbands to follow; but search, nevertheless. It is so important to study your Word and search to find good sound writers, if necessary, to use as resources and examples of correct and godly guides to proper conduct.

The above Scriptures provides husbands with guidelines for living with their wives. The Apostle Paul instructs men to live considerately with their wives. To give you a better sense of what it means to behave considerately, look at the following synonyms: thoughtfully, kindly, understandingly, caringly, selflessly, attentively, sympathetically, respectfully, and solicitously. These are words that could be used in place of living considerately with your wife. Each one of these words is thought provoking with challenging particulars requiring us to review and evaluate our treatment of our wives. Let us remember that God created the marriage institution to be a blessing to all involved and a means for both husband and wife to serve Him better with joy and fulfillment.

Living a godly life requires intelligent recognition of the challenges presented in the marriage relationship. Apostle Paul reminds us that our wives may be physically weaker than we are but are to be honored, and are in no way inferior in the eyes of God (and should not be to men) regarding access to the grace and spiritual benefits as a joint heir of Jesus Christ. As men being God's designated leader in the home, therefore, we must treat our wives with respect. Jesus makes it clear in Matthew 5:23-24 that if we have an issue with our brother or sister that we need to resolve it before coming to God.

Matthew 5:23-24 *(NIV) "Therefore, if you are offering your gift at the altar and there remember that your brother or sister has something against you, leave your gift there in front of the altar. First go and be reconciled to them; then come and offer your gift."*

What are the consequences of not intelligently recognizing and considerately living with our wives? Our prayers will be hindered or rendered ineffective. Pray and ask God to help you assess your conduct toward your wife and to assist you in aligning your lifestyle to please Him in honoring your wife today.

DAY SEVENTY-SEVEN
The Heart of the Matter
(Adrian)

Psalm 139:23-24 *(ESV) Search me, O God, and know my heart! Try me and know my thoughts! And see if there be any grievous way in me, and lead me in the way everlasting!*

In your life activities and your marriage relationship, do you sometimes find yourself asking why do the same issues seem to reoccur over and over again? If you are like me you talk to yourself and say, "You are smarter than this," and maybe you just need to let it go as the popular song out recently says. Do you find yourself struggling to control certain behaviors, having success for only a limited span of time? Do you find it unbelievable that you are back fighting the same habits, matters, and concerns that were fought not so long ago?

I believe that the behaviors or challenges that truly have meaning and need to be resolved are issues that also matter to God. We can sometimes, through determination and great concern, modify our performance or comportment for a moment; but real change can only be achieved from heart-centered actions. In the Scripture above, David asked God to search his heart, to know, and try his thoughts. David trusted God enough to invite Him to search his heart to determine if there was anything that might grieve or cause friction between him and God. David's desire was to stay in the path of everlasting life and fellowship with God.

If you will read the entire Psalm 139, you will note that David had already confessed that God knows everything there is to know about him. He declared that God knew his thoughts before they were even formulated in his mind, so what was David asking God to do for him? He was asking God to help him see his *own* heart and acknowledge where the true correction needed to be made and not just the outward appearance. Many times, our spouses will forgive our actions because they have seen our hidden hearts and love us for the person not always displayed. David knew that the reason he could not consistently perform as desired was because his heart needed to be changed and his direction amended.

If you truly want to love your spouse the way God has defined it in His Word, you are going to need a heart adjustment. This heart correction can only be accomplished with the help of God. Ask God to help you see your heart as the source of your inability to consistently love, forgive, have patience, be long suffering, and share God's gift with others. When you ask God for help, then you will begin to see, through the events and challenges of life and relationships, the uncovering of heart issues that need modifying. You will realize that God is the only force that can assist you to change you where it really counts, your heart. When your heart is changed, your actions will experience lasting behavior reforms.

Let God love you and reveal to you what He already knows and wants to help you overcome.

DAY SEVENTY-EIGHT
A Peculiar Treasure
(Adrian)

Exodus 19:5 *(KJV) Now therefore, if ye will obey my voice indeed, and keep my covenant, then ye shall be a peculiar treasure unto me above all people: for all the earth is mine:*

1 Peter 2:9 *(KJV) But ye are a chosen generation, a royal priesthood, an holy nation, a peculiar people; that ye should shew forth the praises of him who hath called you out of darkness into his marvelous light;*

God declared that the people of Israel, and later those who accepted His gift of salvation through Jesus Christ, are a peculiar people or treasure to Him. The word peculiar used here means special in a valued and honored way as a jewel of great price. God, who is a covenant-keeping God, was selecting a people as His partner for a covenant relationship in one of His sovereign acts. God could have chosen any nation or people since all the earth is His, but He chose Israel. This was a covenant based upon obedience and faith in God and His expressed word. If we, as His chosen people, will allow Him to assist us in complying with His Word, God will bless or endow us with kindness and inexplicable favor beyond our ability to request or mentally fathom. The point is that God made a choice and defined these covenant people as a special treasure to Himself.

Marriage is a covenant between you and your selected mate in which you promise to love, honor, protect, obey, and to exclusively yield yourself to as long as you both shall live. This covenant, for most of us, was conducted in the presence of witnesses, but the most important witness was God. God's desire in making covenant with Israel, and now us, was to bless and protect them as only He could. In our marriages, let's comprehend that our mates should and can be *our* peculiar treasures to bless and be blessed by. They are treasures special to us in the sense that we honor them and value their voluntary commitment to pursuing life together as companions. There should be no greater allegiance, (second only to God) that exists in our life.

The challenge for all covenant partners is to understand and, aggressively, implement the conditions of our voluntary agreements. Review the promises made in your wedding ceremony and purpose to do your best to fulfill them and cherish your spouse. The greatest aspect of being in covenant with God is that He is committed to help you be a success at keeping, not only *His* Word, but yours. Just imagine yourself finally realizing your position as God's peculiar treasure and also permitting Him to cause you to express, every day, that your mate is your personal peculiar treasure to be valued, loved and honored.

DAY SEVENTY-NINE
An "Unobscured" View
(Pam)

I Corinthians 13:12 *(NLT) Now we see things imperfectly, like puzzling reflections in a mirror, but then we will see everything with perfect clarity.*

We recently moved to a very beautiful area that is surrounded by mountains, and the views are gorgeous! Because it's a new neighborhood, lots of construction is going on, and little by little, our beautiful view is becoming obscured. As interesting as the other new homes may appear, they pale in comparison to the vistas that our mountains afford.

What happens when our view gets obstructed? We no longer see what once inspired us, and it becomes easy to forget what was even there in the first place. That's what happens to our marriages, sometimes.

We start out with such fresh energy and hopefulness. We say, "Our marriage is going to be the best one ever!" Suddenly, problems arise that we weren't expecting. The money gets tight, the bills become due, illness may set in, etc. Soon we find ourselves depressed or at each other's throats, and forget all about the joy and excitement of our wedding day. We no longer see the beauty we once saw in each other. What happens next is that we completely forget about God's promises for peace and contentment; so we take on a masked view of life, marriage and God. We can no longer see with any clarity.

How can this be avoided? If we make a conscious effort every day to stay aware of God's goodness and remain thankful for His extraordinary care of us, we will always have an unobscured view of Him. With a view that is not hindered by circumstances, we are more capable of dealing with life's curve balls because we are trusting in the One who is always looking out for us.

There are times when I look out from our back window, I not only see the other houses in the way but thick clouds have rolled in and the mountains seem completely gone. Intellectually, I know it's just temporary, but it still feels a bit disconcerting. That's how it can seem when all hell seems to break loose in our homes. Our heads tell us that it will never get better, but our faith can tell us the truth: that things will change as we trust Father God.

My prayer is that you will keep your eyes open to see all the wonderful things God has for you in your life and in your marriage. Isaiah 64:4 tells us (NLT) "For since the world began, no ear has heard and no eye has seen a God like you, who works for those who wait for him!" I Corinthians 2:9 (KJV) says it this way, "But as it is written, Eye hath not seen, nor ear heard, neither have entered into the heart of man, the things which God hath prepared for them that love him."

DAY EIGHTY
Listen
(Adrian)

Amos 3:3 *(NLT) 3 Can two people walk together without agreeing on the direction?*

In order to have success in your marriage relationship, you must walk in agreement with your spouse. I can hear many of you saying, "That is easier said than done in my home." There have been many books written on communication but I just want to concentrate on one aspect of the communication formula: listening.

In the Scripture above, the word agreement is the essential component of two people being able to walk together. According to the Merriam-Webster Dictionary, agreement is: "harmony of opinion, action or character; an agreement as to a course of action". The truth is that in order to achieve common goals and objectives, agreement must take place. My contention is that agreement will not occur, even in the presence of an abundance of talking, without active listening.

Active listening is rooted in a desire to hear the heart, intent, and desire of the speaker, to allow true communication to take place. True communication allows one to understand the intended meaning of the communicator. We must make the decision to listen with the objective of gaining insight into the desires and goals of our mates. In our marriage relationships, listening is paying attention to the things your spouse says during the day to obtain understanding.

In so many instances, we are speaking, but there is no recognition that the words spoken are received and valued. This may be as simple as when your spouse says that she is tired or overwhelmed and you ask if there is anything you can do to help. You can let her know that you have indeed heard her and volunteer to wash dishes, work with children, or postpone a planned activity in response to what was shared. It may be as simple as noticing the way your spouse answers yes or no. We often find couples saying that their mate doesn't communicate, but the question may really be: Are you paying attention? Not listening can become a detrimental habit that impedes the agreement process in your marriage. When you decide to make the effort to actually listen to one another, the level of the content's importance and communication will increase.

In order for you and your spouse to walk together in agreement, you must first learn to listen to each other. When your spouse knows that you are listening, you may be surprised by the effort he will expend to come to your agreed-upon goals and direction for your lives. Only through listening to God and each other can your marriage relationship arrive at the desired destination.

DAY EIGHTY-ONE
Are You Listening?
(Pam)

Genesis 20:10-12 *(NLT) And Abraham took the knife and lifted it up to kill his son as a sacrifice to the LORD. At that moment the angel of the LORD shouted to him from heaven, "Abraham! Abraham!" "Yes," he answered. "I'm listening." "Lay down the knife," the angel said. "Do not hurt the boy in any way, for now I know that you truly fear God. You have not withheld even your beloved son from me."*

You may be scratching you head about now and wondering what this passage of Scripture could possibly have to do with marriage. I'm glad you asked.

If you recall the story of Abraham and his son, Isaac, you will remember that after years of believing God, Abraham finally received the blessing of a promised son. This was the son in whom he took great delight and loved; but to Abraham's dismay, God asked him to sacrifice Isaac. Although very difficult, Abraham was obedient, believing that God would somehow bring deliverance. And so, the story progressed until Abraham and Isaac were at the place of sacrifice, Mt. Moriah.

To me, one of the most pertinent aspects of this account is that just as Abraham was about to strike his son with the knife, the angel of the Lord called out to him, and Abraham replied, "I'm listening." He was, of course, instructed to lay down the knife and do his son no harm. He obeyed his instructions.

What if Abraham had not heard the angel of the Lord? Or even worse, what if he had heard Him and decided to ignore it. That account would have had a different ending for sure!

My question to you is, how often have you heard God's voice in relationship to your marriage? I know that He is constantly speaking to you about how to treat one another, how to honor one another, how to love one another as *He* does. Are you ignoring Him and doing things your own way?

Listen carefully to the voice of the Lord. Please don't ignore His promptings. There are serious consequences for doing that. Everything He admonishes and even commands us to do is for our good. Trust Him enough to obey Him. I promise that He will make the end of your story a glorious one!

DAY EIGHTY-TWO
"Is'n" With My Best Bud
(Pam)

Proverbs 10:19 *(NLT) In the multitude of words sin is not lacking, But he who restrains his lips is wise.*

"I don't want to be married just to be married. I can't think of anything lonelier than spending the rest of my life with someone I can't talk to, or worse, someone I can't be silent with." (Mary Ann Shaffer, The Guernsey Literary and Potato Peel Pie Society)

One of the most enjoyable aspects to being married, for me, is having an in-house best friend. I've written, in the past, a lot about friendship in marriage, but I want to explore one more concept, and that is the idea of learning how to be comfortable in each other's presence.

I know people who feel the need to always fill any quiet, dead space with words. Neither I nor my husband have that characteristic. We are very cool with just sitting and not saying a word to each other. Have you ever been out to dinner and watched couples who don't speak to each other? What's the typical impression? It's that they probably are no longer in love and have very little to say anymore, right? It may be very true; or it's very possible that they are simply comfortable in each other's presence, and words are just not necessary.

There are times when Adrian and I talk about everything under the sun: the kids, church, music, books, TV, etc. We can laugh and have a good time and also have very robust discussions, but there are times when we experience something we call "is'n". It's when we just "is". I know that's such poor grammar, but it best describes that state when we don't need to talk but are simply enjoying one another's company. One may be reading, or writing, or even playing a game on an electronic device. Occasionally, we may glance up from what we are doing just to exchange a smile or blow a kiss, but the point is that neither of us feels the urgency to fill the air with words. We just "is", and it's great.

If you and your mate feel uncomfortable in silence, try practicing not talking. Of course, if you already *never* talk, there is obviously a more serious issue that needs to be addressed. However, if it is your practice to always feel the need to take a peaceful moment and interrupt it with verbiage, think better of it, and, instead, learn to enjoy just listening to each other breathe.

DAY EIGHTY-THREE
Confidence
(Adrian)

1 John 5:14-15 *Now this is the confidence that we have in Him, that if we ask anything according to His will, He hears us. And if we know that He hears us, whatever we ask, we know that we have the petitions that we have asked of Him.*

The Scriptures quoted above give us insight into how to have confidence in an age of great uncertainty and insecurity. The confidence the Scripture is speaking about is confidence in our Father God. In a time when you are, very possibly, able to see anything your imagination can conceive yet knowing that it is nothing more than the creation of cinematic ingenuity, we are told that we can have confidence – not in what we see but in our God.

When we look at the state of the economy and the decline of so much of humanity around us, it is difficult, at times, to gather and maintain our confidence and assurance of the outcomes promised to us by God. You may look at your marriage and family situation and wonder, "How is this going to work out?" We need to know that the enemy of our faith and confidence, Satan, is constantly trying to distract and discourage us with frightening action scenes played out in our lives that appear to contradict God's promises to His people. The confidence that we can have comes from knowing what the will of God is for our lives and believing He is faithful to keep His promise.

The will of God is recorded in the Word of God; and as we confront situations in life, we can have confidence in God to do what He has promised. We are told to ask, and it will be given to us; but our confidence must be established and secured in knowing that what we are asking is God's will and that He hears us. That is not to say that every situation is specifically defined but every character and intent of God's will is defined in the Word. We know that God instituted marriage and told mankind to be fruitful and multiply. God has made provision for redemption, salvation, healing, health, and wholeness in the sacrifice of His Son Jesus Christ.

When we know the will of God and conform our request to that will, we know that we are heard by Him. Our confidence should soar in a God who is faithful and has made known to us His desires for our lives. Be confident that the challenges of your marriage, family, and life can be confidently addressed and conquered through knowing and embracing the will of God found in His word.

DAY EIGHTY-FOUR
When the Lights Go Out
(Adrian)

Proverbs 3:5-6 *Trust in the Lord with all your heart, and lean not on your own understanding; In all your ways acknowledge Him, and He shall direct your paths.*

Many times, in our walk with the Lord, we find ourselves in situations that puzzle us and may even frighten us. Sometimes, it's as though, somehow, someone has turned the lights off in our lives; and we are plunged into what seems like utter darkness. The darkness can concern so many areas of our lives such as: health, marital discord, finances, parental effectiveness, and maybe even our relationship with God.

The Word of God should always be our compass that will bring us home to the love and safety of God who said "I will never leave you nor forsake you" (Hebrews 13:5). When it appears that a light in our life has gone out, remember God's promise to never leave us. All He asks is for us to trust Him even when we don't understand the situation. We must remember that God loves us and is committed to our salvation and deliverance, both now and throughout eternity.

These times of darkness are like being locked in a dark room in which your captor informs you that there is no way out. But, if we remember God's demonstrated love and promises of loyalty to us, we will trust Him and acknowledge Him. What do I mean? We will stand in the dark room and begin to feel for the walls believing that there is a door of escape supernaturally provided by God. We will keep acknowledging and trusting God until the door is discovered and opened. While you wait for the door to open, you will feel in the darkness for a light switch to provide illumination in your space.

When the lights go out, believe God to restore and guide you to His lighted shelter.

DAY EIGHTY-FIVE
Be kind to One Another
(Adrian)

Ephesians 4:31-32 *(NLT) Get rid of all bitterness, rage, anger, harsh words, and slander, as well as all types of evil behavior. Instead, be kind to each other, tenderhearted, forgiving one another, just as God through Christ has forgiven you.*

As Christians, we sometimes make great and extreme efforts to represent Christ to the world around us. To our friends, coworkers, and strangers we make concerted jesters and accommodations to be personable, kind and good natured. The Scripture above serves as an excellent encouragement and directive to be all these things and more through the Spirit of God who dwells within us. What I would like to challenge you to do is to start your practice of kindness in your home with your spouse and family.

Somehow, we have neglected to follow the instructions from Ephesians 4 in our relations with our spouses and other family members. Bitterness, rage, anger, harsh words and slander must be eliminated from our homes. The amicable nature that we display, often outside the home, must have its roots within our renewed spirit and be shared with those closest to us as well as with rest of the body of Christ and the world.

God directs us to be kind and tenderhearted to each other, but this will require forgiving one another. The challenge in our homes is that we have so many opportunities to forgive those so close and well known by us. The key, though, is to remember that we can forgive because we are forgiven. God forgave us knowing every detail of our actions, thoughts and intentions. God loves and forgives us knowing all, not just what we say or present visually. God has done this because of our acceptance of Christ as Savior and asks us to forgive each other and be kind and tenderhearted.

Show God you truly understand and appreciate His gift of salvation and forgiveness through *your* gift of forgiveness, and loving kindness toward your spouse and family.

DAY EIGHTY-SIX
Don't Worry. Be Happy
(Pam)

John 14:27 *(NLT) "I am leaving you with a gift—peace of mind and heart. And the peace I give is a gift the world cannot give. So don't be troubled or afraid."*

Matthew 6:25a; 27*(NLT)*: **25a** *"That is why I tell you not to worry about everyday life...."* **27** *"Can all your worries add a single moment to your life?"*

I'll bet you immediately started singing that song, didn't you? One can't really help it. It became such a part of our culture for a while. Bobby McFerrin began singing through some of the different circumstances that affected his life and concluded with "Don't worry. Be happy." More easily said than done, I know, but isn't that just what the Scriptures tell us to do?

Despite all the challenges we may face in our lifetime, God never intended for us to walk around filled with stress and anxiety. Jesus left us with a gift of peace of mind and heart, but we have the choice as to whether we will receive it or not. From what I have witnessed for quite some time now, too many Christians have chosen to toss that gift in the trash somewhere. I see an awful lot of wringing of the hands, along with vein-protruding foreheads.

Why do we have such difficulty with worry? My theory is that we believe we can handle our own problems and should only bother God with the really, really tough stuff. Soon we find out that we can't handle it, so we stress out. God wants it all! He desires to assist us with every area of our lives. Peter said in his first letter, *Give all your worries and cares to God, for he cares about you* (I Peter 5:7 NLT). And we certainly cannot forget Paul's admonition, *Don't worry about anything; instead, pray about everything. Tell God what you need, and thank him for all he has done. Then you will experience God's peace, which exceeds anything we can understand. His peace will guard your hearts and minds as you live in Christ Jesus* (Philippians 4:6-7 NLT). Worry is non-productive. It doesn't add anything to your life; in fact, it diminishes it. It interferes with the enjoyment of life as God intended. It causes disease, and it ages you; and it certainly can destroy a marriage.

If you feel like you just can't survive without worrying a little bit, try this exercise I used to share with my class when I taught a module on stress management (I had some expert, professional worriers in that class). Take a situation you are dealing with and think it out to its worst scenario. Now, take that worst case and decide, right there on the spot, what you will do if it actually happens. There, you have dealt with it! Now give it to God and trust Him to handle the outcome for you. I know it sounds too easy, but it is what we must do and what He wants us to do. God has a lot more resources than we do, and if we are willing to trust Him with our very lives, He will never let us down. He is forever faithful! In order to enjoy the abundant life Jesus came to give us, "Don't worry. Be happy."

DAY EIGHTY-SEVEN
Abiding in Peace
(Pam)

Isaiah 30:15, *18 (NLT) This is what the Sovereign Lord, the Holy One of Israel, says: "Only in returning to me and resting in me will you be saved. In quietness and confidence is your strength. So the Lord must wait for you to come to him so he can show you his love and compassion. For the Lord is a faithful God. Blessed are those who wait for his help.*

In the thirtieth chapter of Isaiah, we find that God is rebuking Judah for its self-reliance and desire to look to Egypt for help. The children of Israel had so long been delivered from Egypt yet still looked back there in times of distress.

Isn't that what we do? Sometimes, when things aren't going the way we planned, or we are faced with an abundance of difficulty; we tend to revert back to our old way of thinking, relying on ourselves or others to get us out of trouble instead of remembering where the real solution lies.

Needless to say, marriage is fraught with challenges, giving us many opportunities to make the decision whether to do things our own way or trust that God's way will always, without question, work best. We are so often tested by our pride and selfishness during struggles because it's so easy to shift into protection mode. However, when we decide to trust God instead, we find rest because He is fighting our battles for us. Our stress is relieved and we have peace.

As we release our spouses to God, we find that we no longer have to argue our side of things; we can walk in quietness. This quietness is not a cessation of expression or reasoning but rather a sense of calm as you work through issues. You no longer feel the need to go on the attack because you are confident that, "God's got this!" Instead, you walk in love and remain kind and longsuffering – not easily done in our own strength. Verse 18 tells us that the Lord must wait for us to come to Him so He can show us His love and compassion. God will never force His will on anyone. It's always by choice. We have to choose His peace, His rest, His love. That is where our real strength lies. When we do, we will experience an internal peace that can change the whole atmosphere of our homes.

Abide in peace.

DAY EIGHTY-EIGHT
What are the "Nevers" in Your Marriage?
(Pam)

Proverbs 4:23 *Above all else, guard your heart, for it affects everything you do.*

If you were to think back to when you were a child, you probably remember seeing someone do something and made a conscious decision that you would never do that when you got older. I know I did. I use to watch my father sit on a sofa, and fall asleep with a cigarette in his mouth. I watched in terror, praying that he wakes up before he set our whole house on fire. I knew then that smoking would never be a part of my life. I kept that promise to myself and was not the least bit swayed by peer pressure.

After assessing the damage that we have seen in others' relationships, or even our own, we need to make a determination that there are certain things we will either never do or never do again in our marriages. Your list can be as long or as short as you want, but you need a list. And it's something I recommend you do together.

I'll get you started with some of the things on Adrian's and my list:

- We will never go to bed angry.
- We will never criticize each other in public.
- We will never make each other the brunt of a joke.
- We will never stop doing "loving things" even when we're mad.
- We will never put each other down – ever!

I can guarantee you this: Satan will test you to see if you mean what you declare. Don't be dissuaded by that. The greater one lives on the inside of you and will give you the strength to be fully committed to your stance (I John 4:4).

Now, what's on your list? Having a determined heart not to hurt the one you love keeps a whole lot of things, including our attitudes, in check. It helps us to think twice before we let just "any old thing" come out of our mouths. We become less careless and more vigilant to demonstrate love in our actions.

It may take some practice; and if you find that you violate your "never again list", gently (I said, *gently*) remind each other of your promise and get back on track – and quickly walk in forgiveness.

DAY EIGHTY-NINE
When the Music Fades
(Pam)

Song of Solomon 1:15-16 *(NASB) How beautiful you are, my darling, How beautiful you are! Your eyes are like doves. How handsome you are, my beloved, And so pleasant!*

Have you noticed when you are watching a movie or television program, that there is always some kind of music to accompany a particular scene? Think back to when it was a romantic encounter. It was usually the music that made it seem more dramatic. Generally, there is little, if any, dialog – just music. Have you ever tried to imagine that scene without music? It would be very flat and lifeless, wouldn't it?

Many times, when our relationships are flat and lifeless, it's because the music is fading. It's like someone is watching our life on a screen, and someone turned the volume down so low that you cannot hear the music any longer.

Each of our marriages has its own musical sound. It's the joy of the relationship. How familiar we are with the phrase, "They're playing our song." What was your song? - something romantic and soothing, no doubt. Is that song fading? Is it difficult to hear amidst all the clamor of your hectic life?

We recently met a couple who had been married nearly 30 years. We found ourselves observing their interaction with each other. Afterwards, we discussed it. We both recognized that there was something very sterile about their relationship. It was obvious that they had a measure of respect for each other, and that they probably get along fine. Still, there was something missing. There was no spark – nothing to tell us how they felt about each other. It was not obvious that they were in love. Their music was gone.

Now, do your own assessment. Has your music faded? Do you find that you no longer laugh together, hold hands neither privately nor publicly? Do you not exchange loving glances or smiles across a room? You know, the way you behaved when you were madly in love. Of course, we mature and settle down a bit, but there should still be remnants.

Perhaps someone simply needs to reach over, take the remote and crank up the volume. Or even better, fall on your knees together and ask God to help you reignite your relationship. He is not only the Creator of love, He *is* love; and I promise He wants you to enjoy it.

DAY NINETY
Cut Your Mate Some Slack
(Pam)

1 Corinthians 1:3 *Grace to you and peace from God our Father and the Lord Jesus Christ.*

This is just one of numerous verses in letters written by Apostle Paul to the various churches in which he began his salutation with the phrase, "Grace to you and peace..." Note that every time it was used, it was always used in the same order: grace first then peace. This is significant because grace is the source of peace.

Grace is God's unmerited favor. It is an act of kindness, courtesy, or clemency; a reprieve. When God extended His grace towards us, He lavished His favor on us that we did not merit or deserve.

When we extend that same grace to others, we experience peace. When we extend grace to our mates, we allow them a reprieve or a pardon from the consequences of an action that we may not like. There are many times we just need to give them the grace to mess up and be okay with that.

Sometimes, we are just too hard on each other and we need to "cut our mate some slack". When you cut someone some slack, you are willing to back off a little bit, quit being so demanding or strict and give them a little room to move around and afford them a little freedom.

God gives us room to blow it. Yes, He wants us to get it right, but He knows we won't always. He doesn't turn away from us or withhold His love from us. He's right there to help us get back on track. Can we not give that same grace to each other? If we truly love, it's the least we can do. When we grant grace, we find peace.

End notes

Chapter 1
[1] Hinderson, p.10.

Chapter 2
[1] Merriam-Webster, "Fainthearted," p.449.
[2] Hinderson, p. 9.

Chapter 3
[1] Wheat, p.26

Chapter 4
[1] Wheat, p.32.
[2] Keefauver, p.35.
[3] Ibid.
[4] Ibid.
[5] Hinderson, p.9.

Chapter 6
[1] Meier, p.31.
[2] Ibid, p.35.
[3] Chapman, p.10.

Chapter 7
[1] Wheat, p.111.

Chapter 9
[1] Keefauver, p.29.
[2] Ibid
[3] Ibid, p.74.
[4] Ibid
[5] Henry, p.1297.

Chapter 10
[1] Mayhall, p.167.
[2] Ibid, p.169.
[3] Merriam-Webster, "manage," p.754.
[4].Mayhall, p.170.
[5].Ibid, p.175.

Chapter 11
[1] Mayhall, p.187.
[2] Merriam-Webster, "Submission," p.1244.
[3] Mayhall, p.191.
[4] Christenson, p.37.

Chapter 12
[1] Clark, p.33.
[2] Merriam-Walker, "agreement," p.26.

Chapter 13
[1] Strongs, "Greek" entry # 2845, p. 42
[2] Wheat, p.72.

Day 4
[1]Caldwell

Day 7
[1]Keefauver p. 63

Day 48
[1]Keefauver p.9

Day 66
[1]Bucknell

References

Chapman, Gary. The Five Love Languages: How to Express Heartfelt Commitment to Your Mate. Chicago: Northfield Publishing, 1992.

Christenson, Larry. The Christian Family. Minneapolis: Bethany Fellowship Inc, 1970

Clarke, David. Men Are Clams, Woman Are Crowbars: Understand Your Differences And Make Them Work. Urichsville: Promise Press, 1998.

Henry, Matthew. Commentary on the Whole Bible. Grand Rapids: Zondervan Publishing House, 1961.

Hinderson, Edward E. The Total Family. Wheaton: Tyndale House Publishers Inc., 1980.

Keefauver, Larry and Judi. Seventy Seven Irrefutable Truths of Marriage. Gainsville: Bridge-Logos Publishers, 2002.

Mayhall, Jack and Carole. Marriage Takes More Than Love. Colorado Springs: Navpress, 1978

Meier, Paul and Richard. Family Foundations: How to Have a Happy Home. Grand Rapids: Baker Book

House, 1981.

Merriam-Webster. Merriam-Webster's Collegiate <u>Dictionary, Eleventh Edition</u>. Springfield: Merriam-Webster, Incorporated, 2003.

Strong, James. <u>Strong's Exhaustive Concordance</u>. Grand Rapids: Baker Book House, 1981.

Wheat, Ed. <u>Love Life for Every Married Couple</u>. Grand Rapids: Zondervan Publishing House, 1961.

Bucknell, Paul and Linda. <u>Building a Great Marriage! Finding Faith, Forgiveness and Friendship.</u> Paul J. Bucknell, 2002,2009,2013,

Caldwell, Robert. "The Difficult and Compelling Art of Forgiving." Psychsight.com

Recommended Reading

Harley, Jr., Willard. <u>His Needs, Her Needs: Building an Affair-Proof Marriage</u>. Grand Rapids: Fleming H. Revell, 1986.

Wheat, Ed and Gaye. <u>Intended for Pleasure: Sex Technique and Sexual Fulfillment in Christian Marriage</u>. Grand Rapids: Fleming H. Revell, 1977.

LaHaye, Tim and Beverly. <u>The Act of Marriage: The Beauty of Sexual Love</u>. Grand Rapids: Zondervan, 1976.

Slattery, Dr, Juli. <u>No More Headaches: Enjoying Sex and Intimacy in Marriage.</u> Julianna Slattery, 2009.

www.ingramcontent.com/pod-product-compliance
Lightning Source LLC
Chambersburg PA
CBHW031407290426
44110CB00011B/295